DK EYEWITNESS T

TOP10

R

PAUL BERNHARDT

LOOK FOR:
- ___ Books
- ___ Booklets
- ___ CDs
- ___ Charts
- ___ DVDs
- ___ Inserts
- _1_ Maps
- ___ Music parts
- ___ _____
- ___ _____

Top 10 Azores Highlights

The Top 10 of Everything

CONTENTS

Azores
Area by Area

Streetsmart

Within each Top 10 list in this book, no hierarchy of quality or popularity is implied. All 10 are, in the editor's opinion, of roughly equal merit.
  Throughout this book, floors are referred to in accordance with European usage; i.e., the "first floor" is the floor above ground level.

Front cover and spine *Caldeira das Sete Cidades seen from Vista do Rei viewpoint, São Miguel*
Back cover *Igreja de Santa Maria Madalena in Pico town centre*
Title page *A sperm whale off the Pico coast, with Montanha do Pico in the background*

Welcome to
The Azores

The nine islands of the Azores are scattered in the Atlantic Ocean, 1,500 km (932 miles) west of Portugal's mainland. Thanks to its mild climate, this archipelago offers a wealth of outdoor and adventure tourism options. It is also noted for its biodiversity, and is packed with historical and cultural charm. These Portuguese islands have something for everyone, and with Eyewitness Top 10 Azores, they're yours to explore.

Clustered into three areas – the Eastern Group duo of **São Miguel** and **Santa Maria**, the Central Group quintet of **Terceira**, **Graciosa**, **São Jorge**, **Pico** and **Faial**, and the Western Group pairing of **Flores** and **Corvo** – these islands differ widely. The Azores' volcanic origins are evident in the massive **Sete Cidades** crater and soaring **Montanha do Pico** – Portugal's highest mountain. **Capelinhos** volcano is a reminder of nature's destructive forces while **Algar do Carvão** mesmerizes with its grandeur. The **Furnas** hot springs are equally compelling. Pristine biosphere reserves shield flora and fauna, including the rare **Azores bullfinch**. Offshore waters harbour a variety of sea life, where some of the best **whale and dolphin watching** in the world can be enjoyed.

There's a richness of culture, from the UNESCO-listed **Angra do Heroísmo** and **Pico Island vineyards** to the **Festas do Espírito Santo** and many other festivals. The Azores are also wonderfully outdoorsy. **Walking** and **hiking** trails crisscross every island. Watersports choices include **sailing**, **kayaking** and plenty of outstanding **dive sites**.

Whether you're visiting for a weekend or a week, our Top 10 guide brings together the best of everything this far-flung destination has to offer. It gives you tips throughout, from the best **bars** and **restaurants** to the most rewarding **shopping**, plus four easy-to-follow itineraries, designed to tie together a clutch of sights in a short space of time. Add inspiring photography and detailed maps, and you've got the essential pocket-sized travel companion. **Enjoy the book, and enjoy the Azores**.

Clockwise from top: Angra do Heroísmo marina, Igreja de Santa Cruz in Praia da Vitória, statue of Christ in Horta's Igreja de São Salvador, the picturesque Caldeira das Sete Cidades, Risso's dolphins, windmills at Ponta da Espalamaca, pink azalea at Lagoa das Furnas

Exploring the Azores

From UNESCO-listed vineyards and crater lakes to world-class whale watching and hot springs, the Azores are rich in natural beauty. Here are some ideas to make the most of your time in the archipelago. A two-day jaunt on São Miguel is enough time to explore all the "must-sees". Stay for a week and indulge in an exciting island-hop – the "triangle" that is Pico, Faial and São Jorge.

Pico's vineyards are protected by UNESCO as a World Heritage Site.

Horta marina on Faial is the primary port of call for transatlantic yachts.

Two Days on São Miguel

Day ❶
MORNING
Enjoy coffee and home-made pastries at **Louvre Michaelense** (see p59) in **Ponta Delgada** (see pp12–13). Later, explore **Gruta do Carvão** (see p12).
AFTERNOON
Marvel at the incredible **Caldeira das Sete Cidades** (see pp14–15), where the views from **Miradouro da Vista do Rei** (see p14) are outstanding. Stop for coffee and cake in the village, then go kayaking (see p50) on the lakes.

Day ❷
MORNING
Have breakfast at **Mascote** (see p74), then head to **Cerâmica Vieira** (see p71) to see traditional pottery. Continue to **Vila Franca do Campo** (see p70).
AFTERNOON
Scenic **Vale das Furnas** (see pp18–19) deserves an entire afternoon, but lunch first at **Tony's** (see p75).

A Seven-Day Island-Hop: Faial, Pico and São Jorge

Day ❶
Spend the day in **Horta** (see pp26–7), starting with the **Museu da Horta** (see p26). Admire the murals at **Marina da Horta** (see p26) and have lunch at **Peter Café Sport** (see p96). Afterwards, tour **Casa dos Dabney** (see p26) and nearby **Aquário de Porto Pim** (see p27). End the day with dinner at **Genuíno** (see p54).

Day ❷
Join a pre-booked excursion with **OceanEye** (see p94) and see Azorean marine life up-close. Later, enjoy seafood in the restaurants located at the marina. Visit **Capelinhos** volcano (see pp28–9) and see the impressive subterranean Centro de **Interpreteção do Vulcão dos Capelinhos** (see p29). Shop for souvenirs at **Escola de Artesanato do Capelo** (see p94) on the way back.

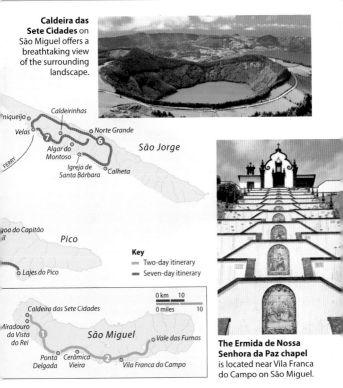

Caldeira das Sete Cidades on São Miguel offers a breathtaking view of the surrounding landscape.

The Ermida de Nossa Senhora da Paz chapel is located near Vila Franca do Campo on São Miguel.

Key
— Two-day itinerary
■■ Seven-day itinerary

Day ❸
Take a ferry across the channel to **Pico** (see pp88–91) and **Madalena** (see p93), your base for the next three days. Walk along the **Vinhas da Criação Velha Trail** (see p33). Pass by UNESCO-listed vineyards, then visit the windmill. Return in time for supper at **Ancoradouro** (see p55).

Day ❹
Head to **Lajes do Pico** (see p93) for a pre-booked **whale-watching** trip (see pp16–17). After lunch at **Pastelaria Aromas & Sabores** (see p96), visit the engrossing **Museu dos Baleeiros** (see p39). Finish the day over a glass of wine at **Cella Bar** (see p97).

Day ❺
Begin with the **Museu do Vinho** (see p32). Afterwards, join a guided tour with wine tastings at the **Centro de Interpretação da Paisagem da Cultura da Vinha da Ilha do Pico** (see p33). Hike the **Lagoa do Capitão Trail** (see p93) under **Montanha do Pico** (see p42).

Day ❻
Catch the ferry to **São Jorge** (see pp88–91) and explore **Velas** (see p92). Take a guided tour of the **Uniqueijo** cheese factory (see p92), then head to Norte Grande and lunch at **Almicar** (see p97). Cross the island to **Calheta** (see p92) before skirting the coast to **Igreja de Santa Bárbara** (see p40).

Day ❼
Pack a picnic and take a taxi drop to the **Caldeirinhas–Norte Grande** walk (see p46). Confirm the pick-up for afterwards. Later in the day, explore **Algar do Montoso** (see p92) on a pre-booked caving expedition. Finish with dinner at **Café Açor** (see p96).

These itineraries focus on four of the nine Azorean islands

Top 10 Azores Highlights

The striking volcanic landscape
of Capelinhos on the Faial coast

🔟 Azores Highlights

A tranquil mid-Atlantic setting, dramatic volcanic scenery and splendid eco diversity make the Azores a compelling choice for outdoor enthusiasts and adventurous travellers. Each of the nine islands has its own distinctive character, and these standout attractions show why this remote Portuguese outpost has become one of the world's most desirable tourist destinations.

① Ponta Delgada

The largest town in the Azores, Ponta Delgada is São Miguel's vibrant, ocean-facing hub and an ideal introduction to the archipelago (see pp12–13).

② Caldeira das Sete Cidades

This enormous volcanic crater hugs two idyllic lakes, and the views from its rim are awe-inspiring (see pp14–15).

Velas • • Norte Grand
Capelinhos ⑧ *Faial* Manadas • Calheta
Horta Paisagem da Cultura ⑩ da Vinha da Ilha do Pico
⑦
Madalena • • São Roque do Pico
Candelária • *Pico* • Pié
São Mateus • Lajes do Pico •

③ Whale and Dolphin Watching

The Azores are one of the world's top whale- and dolphin-watching hot spots, with some 28 cetacean species seen here (see pp16–17).

⑤ Angra do Heroísmo

UNESCO has declared Angra a World Heritage Site, such is the splendour of its Renaissance buildings (see pp20–21).

④ Vale das Furnas

This is the archipelago's geothermal crowd-pleaser, with hot springs and fumaroles (see pp18–19).

Diving Spots 6

Luminous blue waters and glittering shoals of Atlantic and tropical fish distinguish the region as one of the richest marine habitats on the planet (see pp24–5).

Horta 7

A mid-ocean haven for yachts, Faial's port town boasts the world's largest collection of maritime paintings – all of them daubed on the marina walls and pier (see pp26–7).

Terceira
Lajes
Algar do Carvão 9
Santa Bárbara ● ● Praia da Vitória
São Mateus ●
5 Angra do Heroísmo

São Jorge
● Topo

0 kilometres 20
0 miles 20

Capelinhos 8

The destructive forces of nature are apparent here, the scene of a series of volcanic eruptions and seismic tremors in the late 1950s (see pp28–9).

0 km 15
0 miles 15

2 Caldeira das Sete Cidades
Porto Formoso ● ● Nordeste
Ribeira Grande ●
Candelária ●
São Miguel 4 Vale das Furnas
1 Lagoa ● Povoação
Ponta Delgada ● Vila Franca do Campo

Algar do Carvão 9

A dramatic, 2,000-year-old volcanic blast-hole, this dank, half-lit lava tube widens into a huge subterranean cavern (see pp30–31).

Paisagem da Cultura da Vinha da Ilha do Pico 10

Pico's landscape of volcanic vineyards and the island's centuries-old winemaking tradition are unique, a fact recognized by UNESCO (see pp32–3).

Most of these highlights are concentrated on and around four of the nine Azorean islands

TOP 10 ⭐ Ponta Delgada

The largest town in the Azores, historic Ponta Delgada melds maritime tradition with plenty of cultural clout. Set against a wide, sweeping bay, its impressive black-and-white chapels, churches, monasteries and museums overlook parks and gardens flecked with colour. Centuries of trade between Europe and the New World placed the port at the vanguard of transatlantic commerce. Today, ocean-going cruise ships also line the quay, flying the flags of far-flung nations. Take time to explore this capital and revel in its unhurried lifestyle.

1 Jardim e Palácio de Sant'Ana

This serene botanical garden **(above)** is admired for its flowering shrubs. Notable trees include the Norfolk Island pine and *pohutukawa*.

2 Arruda Açores Pineapple Plantation

Pineapple is a delicacy in the Azores. A tour of the estate takes in the greenhouses, and fruit can be purchased.

3 Igreja Matriz de São Sebastião

Richly sculptured motifs adorn the façade of this splendid 16th-century church. The interior is enriched with cedarwood carvings and hand-glazed *azulejos* (tiles).

4 Gruta do Carvão

Hidden under the town's western outskirts is the island's largest cave system. It is around 250 m (820 ft) long, and a part of it is open to the public.

5 Portas da Cidade

Built of regional stone in 1783, the city gates were originally set against the old harbour wall. Illustrious visitors, including members of the Portuguese royal family, would have passed under the graceful arches of this symbolic entrance **(below)**.

THE AZORES PINEAPPLE

Plated up in restaurants as a tropical fruit dessert, or combined with grilled spicy sausage for a tasty appetizer, pineapple is ubiquitous throughout the Azores. It was introduced from South America in the mid-19th century. São Miguel was favoured as a location for growing this fruit, with greenhouse estates at Fajã de Baixo, near Ponta Delgada, and Vila Franco do Campo.

6 Portas do Mar

A maritime terminal for cruise ships and interisland ferries **(left)**, the multi-functional "Sea Gates" complex also includes a top-notch marina. The quay is lined with shops, cafés and restaurants.

Map of Ponta Delgada

8 Forte de São Brás

This 16th-century fort is a fine example of military architecture. Today, it houses the Museu Militar dos Açores *(see p70)*.

9 Museu Carlos Machado

Inaugurated in 1888, this museum features interesting exhibits such as a cannonball from a sea battle in 1582 *(see p39)*.

10 Igreja do Colégio

The expulsion of the Jesuits in 1760 left the altar of this church only partially gilded. What was done, however, is still magnificent *(see p40)*.

7 Convento e Santuário de Nossa Senhora da Esperança

The Convent of Our Lady of Hope is a sanctuary for a revered piece of sacred art, Ecce Homo **(above)**, embellished with gems and precious metals *(see p41)*.

NEED TO KNOW

Jardim e Palácio de Sant'Ana: **MAP U1**; Rua José Jácome Correia; (296) 301 000; garden open 10am–5pm Tue–Sun; palace open by appointment only; adm €2 (garden), under 14s free, over 65s €1

Arruda Açores Pineapple Plantation: **MAP B6**; Rua Doutor Augusto Arruda, Fajã de Baixo; (296) 384 438; open Jun–Sep: 9am–8pm; Oct–May: 9am–6pm

Gruta do Carvão: **MAP B6**; Rua do Paim; (296) 284 155; open 10am–12:30pm & 2–6pm daily; guided tours 10:30am, 11:30am, 2:30pm, 3:30pm & 4:30pm daily; adm €5, under 5s free, 6–11-year-olds €1, senior citizens €2.50; grutadocarvao.pt

Convento e Santuário de Nossa Senhora da Esperança: **MAP U2**; Praça 5 de Outubro; (296) 284 453; open 5:30–6:30pm daily

Forte de São Brás: **MAP U2**; Avenida Infante Dom Henrique; (296) 304 920; open 10am–6pm Mon–Fri, 10am–1:30pm & 2:30–6pm Sat & Sun; adm €3, concessions, under 12s free

Igreja do Colégio: **MAP U1**; Largo do Colégio; (296) 202 930; adm

■ The Largarta tourist train follows five themed audio city-tour routes: Historical, Heritage, Outskirts, Beach and Gardens.

🔟 ⭐ Caldeira das Sete Cidades

One of the defining natural wonders of the Azores, the volcanic crater of Sete Cidades emerges from São Miguel's northwestern shoulder to dominate the island. With a 12-km (7-mile) circumference, it cups two enchanting lakes, one blue, one green. Sunk into the surrounding landscape is a collection of smaller lakes, droplets compared to their neighbours. A small village sits by the water's edge, a community dwarfed by its location but steeped in tradition – a place where romantic myth prevails *(see p67)*. Take a day out and hike the green walls around this special place. The justifiably famous views will leave you speechless.

THE BIRTH OF "SABRINA"

In 1811 earth tremors shook the coast of São Miguel near Ponta do Escalvaldo, culminating in a submarine volcanic eruption. Four days later, in early June, a new island emerged – a circular cone 2 km (1 mile) in diameter and 100 m (328 ft) tall. Alerted by the explosions, the British sloop *Sabrina* set sail to investigate. The commanding officer planted a Union Jack on the landmass, claiming it for Great Britain and naming it Sabrina. But four months later the island sank, along with Britain's claim on it.

1 Miradouro da Vista do Rei
Named after the 1901 visit of King Dom Carlos, who stood at this overlook to admire the scenery, the viewpoint still affords a regal panorama **(above)**.

2 Loja do Parque da Lagoa das Sete Cidades
The park's shop and visitor centre stocks information about the area's walking trails, its flora and fauna, geology and classified heritage.

3 Lagoa Azul
The larger of the two lakes, the "Blue Lake" has a scattering of well-maintained bungalows and low-key watersports operations along its shores, where visitors can hire kayaks and stand-up paddleboards.

4 Lagoa Verde
The "Green Lake" **(below)** is so named because this side of the crater reflects the sunlight in shades of myrtle, jade and shamrock. To the northwest of the lake is a recreation zone.

Map of Caldeira das Sete Cidades

5 Mosteiros–Ponta do Escalvado–Ginetes–Rabo do Asno Trail

Nearly 12 km (7 miles) in length, this energizing coastal hike skirts the lower outside walls of the caldera and takes in the Ponta do Escalvado **(above)**.

6 Mosteiros

Appreciated for its black sand beach and natural rock pools, this coastal village boasts some excellent seafood restaurants *(see p75)*.

7 Miradouro da Grota do Inferno

The "Hell's Cave" lookout presents the Santiago, Rasa and Azul lakes in one of the Azores' finest natural canvases.

8 Vista do Rei–Sete Cidades Trail

The trail for this pleasant ramble begins at the Vista do Rei viewpoint and snakes around the top of Lagoa Verde.

9 Lagoa do Canário

In spring butterflies can be seen flitting over pretty azaleas as hikers follow the Mata do Canário foot-path to the water's edge.

10 Sete Cidades Village

Nestling at Lagoa Azul's edge is the idyllic village of Sete Cidades. Distinguished by its Neo-Gothic church **(below)**, the secluded hamlet appears cradled by the enormous crater.

NEED TO KNOW

MAP A5

Loja do Parque da Lagoa das Sete Cidades: Module No. 5, Lagoa Azul, Sete Cidades; (296) 249 016; open 9am–4pm daily

■ A pioneer of social and inclusive tourism in the Azores, Cresaçor (Loja Eco-Atlântida, Rua Nova 45; (296) 098 866; Oct–Mar: closed Sun) provides amenities to those with limited mobility or who have learning difficulties. It has an eco-store in Sete Cidades where visitors can rent kayaks and mountain bikes. The company also organizes walking tours and jeep safaris.

■ Lagoa do Canário is a lovely picnic spot.

■ Restaurante São Nicolau is one of the few dining options in Sete Cidades and is convenient for a light meal (Rua da Igreja 20; (296) 295 589).

TOP 10 ★ Whale and Dolphin Watching

Moored between two continents and surrounded by the Atlantic Ocean, the Azores archipelago is one of the world's premier whale- and dolphin-watching destinations. Attracted by the mild, nutrient-rich currents of the Gulf Stream, some 28 species of cetaceans have been sighted here. The majority of these gentle giants arrive early in the year for the warm summer season, escorted by pods of intelligent, lively dolphins. Take an excursion out to sea and admire these creatures in their natural habitat.

WHALE PURSUITS

American whalers, who arrived around 1765, introduced whaling to the Azores. Over the next two centuries, numerous whaling companies were set up. The *cachalote* (sperm whale) was taken frequently, the carcass beached and the blubber melted down for oil. Later the entire animal was used. The mid-20th century saw global whale numbers fall alarmingly and by 1988 whaling had ended in the Azores.

1 Risso's Dolphin

Distinguished by their rounded head and curiously scarred frame, resident populations of Risso's are usually found in deeper water. They can be extremely frisky.

2 Common Bottlenose Dolphin

Seen all year, these sociable and inquisitive animals never fail to please. Their frolicking and high-flying antics elicit applause and smiles as wide as theirs.

3 Atlantic Spotted Dolphin

Cruising into Azorean waters with their calves around June and staying until the end of November, these dolphins (below) gather in their hundreds.

4 Blue Whale

This is the largest animal (above) ever known to have lived on the Earth. Visitors are most likely to see these sleek, agile swimmers off Pico's southern coast, from around March to the beginning of June.

WWW.ESPACOTALASSA.COM

5 Striped Dolphin

Named for the long, striped outline running on either side of the body, this species is found fairly regularly during the summer, autumn and early winter.

6 Sei Whale

Another ocean-going giant and one of the fastest, reaching speeds over 50 kmph (30 mph). Spring is the best time to see them.

7 Fin Whale

Measuring up to 27 m (90 ft), this is the world's second-biggest whale. Slender and solitary, it can be spotted from March to September.

Short-Beaked Common Dolphin 8

This species **(right)** is identified by a distinctive "hourglass" pattern on their flanks. They often gather in groups to bow ride in front of boats.

9 Sperm Whale

Iconic to the Azores, this is the archipelago's most commonly sighted whale **(above)**. Summer months are particularly rewarding, with groups often appearing near the coast off São Miguel, Terceira, Faial and Pico.

10 Short-Finned Pilot Whale

Recognized by its bulbous melon head and dorsal fin located far forward on the body, this whale is in fact a larger member of the dolphin group. They are usually spotted from mid-May to October.

NEED TO KNOW

Espaço Talassa: **MAP N3**; (292) 672 010; www. espacotalassa.com

Futurismo: **MAP V2**; (296) 559 385; www. futurismo.pt

Museu dos Baleeiros: **MAP N3**; Rua dos Baleeiros 13, Lajes do Pico, Pico; (292) 679 340; open summer: 10am–5:30pm Tue–Sun, winter: 9:30am–5pm Tue–Sun; adm €2, 14–25-year-olds €1, under 14s free

Museu de Cachalotes e Lulas: **MAP L2**; Avenida Machado Serpa, Madalena, Pico; open Jun–Sep: 10am–6pm Tue–Fri, 1:30–5pm Sat & Sun, Oct–May: 9am–5pm Mon–Fri; adm

■ The former spotting stations, or *vigias,* now make great land-based whale watching posts.

■ Stay up to date about the world of whales at wwf.panda.org/what_ we_do/endangered_ species/cetaceans.

🔟 ⭐ Vale das Furnas

Draped over a volcanic depression, the Furnas Valley is a vivid landscape moulded within the rim of a colossal caldera. A scenic village and a splendid lake sit on a beautiful valley floor painted every shade of green. Simmering beneath this picturesque veneer, however, is a rumbling underworld of steam and boiling water – the *caldeiras*. Spluttering to the surface, these bubbling and burping hot springs are São Miguel's geothermal crowd-pleasers.

Caldeiras das Furnas

Hot springs belching mud, boiling fumaroles and a rotten-egg odour – Furnas' *caldeiras* are bad tempered and smelly. The largest and the noisiest ones are clustered around the town centre **(right)**.

② Parque Terra Nostra

A botanist's paradise, this historic park has more than 600 varieties of camellias, a collection of rare cycads and pretty amaryllis. Take a stroll on the Avenue of Palms and then a dip in the geothermal pool *(see p45)*.

③ Ermida de Nossa Senhora das Vitórias

On Lake Furnas' southern shore is this Neo-Gothic funerary chapel **(below)**, the final resting place of botanist José do Canto (1820–1898) and his wife Maria. The building itself is closed, but visit the nearby gardens.

NEED TO KNOW

Parque Terra Nostra: **MAP E5**; Largo Marquês da Praia; (296) 549 090; open Apr–Sep: 10am–7pm daily; Oct–Jan: 10am–5pm; Feb & Mar: 10am–5:30pm; adm €8, under 2s free, 3–10-year-olds & over 65s €4; www.parqueterranostra.com

Observatório Microbiano dos Açores: **MAP E5**; Antigo Chalé de Misturas, Caldeiras; (296) 584 765 (call ahead for guided tours and mineral water tastings); open 10am–5pm Tue–Fri, 2:30–6pm Sat & Sun (closed Sep–Jun: Sat); adm €1, over 65s 75 cents, under 17s 50 cents

Poça da Dona Beija: **MAP E5**; Lomba das Barracas; (296) 584 256; open 7am–11pm daily (last adm 10:30pm); adm; pocadadonabeija.com

Centro de Monitorização e Investigação das Furnas: **MAP E6**; Rua Lagoa das Furnas; (296) 584 436; open Jun–Sep: 10am–6pm daily; Oct–May: 10am–5pm Tue–Sun; adm €3, over 65s €1.50, under 16s free

■ Tony's is renowned for its hospitality and *cozido das Furnas (see p75)*.

■ Look for the snack kiosk in the car park selling *milho cozido* (corn on the cob), boiled in sacks suspended in the *caldeiras'* waters.

5 Poça da Dona Beíja

This hot springs complex **(left)** allows visitors to soak in five open-air rock pools fed by a mineral-rich thermal spring. At night the spa is illuminated with spotlights, lending it a romantic appeal.

6 Centro de Monitorização e Investigação das Furnas

This research centre highlights the lake's eco-system and local flora and fauna. Look for the "volcanic bomb", a rare sample of pyroclastic debris from the 1439 Pico do Gaspar eruption.

7 Miradouro do Pico do Ferro

A bird in flight couldn't get a better view of the Furnas Valley. The panorama embraces the lake and the town, which resembles a Lilliputian hamlet from this height.

MINERAL WEALTH

In 1930 eminent Azorean hydrologist Armando Narciso da Cunha (1890–1948) declared Furnas Valley the most exuberant and abundant region of thermal waters in Europe. An incredible 20 different mineral waters gush from the ground in the village. Water from the Água do Padre José fountain, for example, is traditionally used to make thermal teas. However, due to its chemical structure this water causes green tea to turn purple. Coffee anyone?

8 Lagoa das Furnas

The second-largest lake **(below)** on São Miguel is inhabited by a variety of wildfowl, including ring-necked ducks and greater scaups. Hiking the 11-km (7-mile) nature trail around the lake is a great way to spend 3 hours (see p42).

4 Observatório Microbiano dos Açores

Visitors can find answers to all that they want to know about the microbial diversity at OMIC, the educative Microbe Observatory of the Azores.

9 Furnas Village

Sitting in the lap of the valley, Furnas is one of São Miguel's most frequently visited spots. The village's claim to fame is its volcanic heritage, lush gardens and unique gastronomy.

10 Cozido das Furnas

Chicken, beef, pork, spicy *chouriço* sausage, black pudding, yam, sweet potato, carrot, cabbage and kale are cooked below ground for 7 hours to make the most succulent one-pot dish travellers are likely to taste (see p57).

Map of Vale das Furnas

Furnas

Pico do Ferro 570m

Pico do Gaspar 373m

🔟 ⭐ Angra do Heroísmo

A UNESCO World Heritage Site, Angra do Heroísmo's Renaissance old town, scenic bay and pretty gardens make it one of the Azores' most beautiful places. From the 1600s to the mid-19th century, Angra was a port of strategic importance. The age of sail and Portuguese discoveries brought with it wealth and prestige – a prosperity invested in palaces, monasteries and churches. Visitors will enjoy the town's fascinating history and the architecture that defines it.

1 Santíssimo Salvador da Sé

This cathedral is noted for the altar's 18th-century antependium, a superb example of Terceiran tracery. Also look for the lectern crafted from Brazilian jacaranda and inlaid with whale ivory.

2 Rua Direita

The town's most attractive thoroughfare has elegant buildings with colour-trimmed windows and filigree wrought-iron balconies. It takes visitors from the harbour to Praça Velha, the central square.

3 Museu de Angra do Heroísmo

The museum's exhibition **(left)** "From the Sea and the Land... a Story in the Atlantic" delves into the Azores' eventful past. Pieces such as the exquisite 16th-century planetary astrolabe are truly stunning *(see p38)*.

4 Igreja da Misericórdia

The blue façade of this 18th-century church defines Angra's harbour. It stands on the site of the first hospital built in the Azores *(see p40)*.

5 Palácio dos Capitães Generais

The 18th-century Palace of the Captain Generals is complemented by the adjoining Igreja do Santo Inácio de Loyola, which houses one of the best collections of 17th-century Dutch tiles outside the Netherlands **(below)**.

6 Palácio Bettencourt

Noted for its handsome portico, this early-18th-century palace is now a public library. Its archive has a valuable collection of rare books. This literary treasure can be viewed by appointment.

7 Convento de São Gonçalo

Angra's largest and oldest convent is a feast of Baroque and Rococo architecture. The altar is flanked by *azulejos* (tiles) dating from the 18th century *(see p41)*.

JOÃO VAZ CORTE-REAL

João Vaz Corte-Real (1420–96) is credited with the discovery of Newfoundland in 1473 – a landmass that he called "New Land of the Codfish". Appointed Angra's Capitão Donatário in 1474, the new governor was a founding member of the society that supported the construction of the first hospital in the Azores, built in 1492 on a site now occupied by the Igreja da Misericórdia.

Castelo da São João Baptista

8 Created by Filipe II during Spain's annexation of Portugal *(see p36)*, Angra's castle **(right)** houses the first church built after the restoration of the Portuguese monarchy.

Angra do Heroísmo with Monte Brasil in the background

Map of Angra do Heroísmo

Outeiro da Memória

9 The much-reproduced rooftop view of the town, its bay and Monte Brasil beyond is taken near this obelisk. Erected in 1846 in memory of King Dom Pedro IV, it stands on the site of the first fort built in the Azores in 1474.

Jardim Duque da Terceira

10 Teeming with roses, magnolias, cycads and tree ferns, this garden is an urban oasis. The grounds were originally part of the Convento de São Francisco.

NEED TO KNOW

Santíssimo Salvador da Sá: **MAP U4**; Rua da Sé; (295) 217 850; open 10am–5:30pm Mon–Sat, 9am–noon Sun; adm €2, under 16s free

Museu de Angra do Heroísmo: **MAP V3**; Ladeira de São Francisco; (295) 240 800; open Apr–Sep: 10am–6pm Tue–Sun; Oct–Mar: 9:30am–5pm

Tue–Sun; adm €2 (free Sun), over 65s €1, under 14s free

Palácio dos Capitães Generais: **MAP U3**; Rua do Palácio; (295) 402 300; open 10am–5pm Tue–Sun; adm €3, under 14s free

Palácio Bettencourt: **MAP U4**; Rua da Rosa; (295) 401 000; open 9am–5pm Mon–Fri (winter: to 7pm), 2–7pm Sat

Castelo da São João Baptista: **MAP M6**; Monte Brasil; (295) 214 011; open 10am–5pm Mon–Sat

Jardim Duque da Terceira: **MAP V3**; open summer: 8am–midnight daily; winter: 8am–10pm daily

■ A guided cultural walking tour is organized by Angra 2000 (angra2000.com).

Following pages Scenic landscape of Faial dotted with hydrangeas and windmills

TOP10 ⭐ Diving Spots

With their rich marine biodiversity, the Azores offer some of the best diving conditions in the world. High visibility in temperate, crystalline waters and a seafloor sculpted from lava exemplify this vast maritime region. There are nearly 100 diving sites found across the archipelago, each one a veritable underwater wonderland teeming with sea life. The impressive subaquatic landscape features shipwrecks, volcanic seamounts, and warrens of basaltic caves and tunnels. In places, marine reserves and archaeological parks have been established to showcase fragile reefs and the Azores' seafaring heritage. Visitors who dive off the nine islands will have the opportunity to swim with some of nature's greatest marine life.

1 Dori

The wreck of the *Edwin L Drake*, a former Liberty ship **(below)** that was built in the US during World War II and sank off the southern coast of São Miguel in 1964, is a designated subaquatic archaeological park. Much of the stern is still intact. Marine life is abundant on this artificial reef.

2 Ilhéus das Formigas

This outcrop of scattered rock **(above)** 33 nautical miles (60 km) southeast of São Miguel is noted for its rich variety of pelagic fishes. Wait for favourable sea conditions to explore this marine reserve.

3 Gruta dos Enxaréus

The mysterious pirate cave hidden at the foot of cliffs outside Santa Cruz on Flores reveals a submerged cavern, the dark corridors of which are patrolled by beady-eyed stingrays (see p99).

4 Caneiro dos Meros

This dive spot is well known for having the greatest concentration of dusky grouper in the Azores. These fish glide through the archipelago's first and only voluntary marine reserve, in front of Vila do Corvo, Corvo's tiny harbour.

7 Ilhéu do Topo

A protected reserve for birds, Ilhéu do Topo has a fertile ecosystem that extends underwater, where yellowmouth barracuda mingle with barred hogfish **(left)**. The dive site is off the far eastern tip of São Jorge *(see p92)*.

RICH MARINE LIFE IN THE AZORES

The Azores are a marine life hot spot. Nearly 30 of the world's 80-odd cetaceans have been seen here, including humpbacks and minkes. Dolphins scythe the waves, and loggerhead turtles row through the water as manta rays and devil rays glide by. The mid-ocean seamounts attract both blue and whale sharks, and Portuguese man o' wars gather by the thousand. Texturing the seabed are purple sea stars, yellow encrusting anemones, fireworms and nudibranchs. Adding tropical brilliance are parrotfish and wrasses.

5 Gruta e Ilhéu Negro

The best way to enjoy this dive is to make it on a bright and cloudless day. The shards of sunlight beaming through the ice-blue sea will illuminate the entrance to the submerged cave, which is burrowed under Faial's Monte da Guia **(below)**.

6 Naufrágio Terceirense

Exploring the wreck of the *Terceirense* that sank in 1968 outside the port of Praia on Graciosa is rewarded with an array of colourful fish, including canary damsels, rainbow wrasses and parrotfish.

8 Banco D João de Castro

Grey triggerfish and Atlantic bonito are among the sea life found congregating in and around this intriguing submarine volcano, located 35 nautical miles (65 km) from Terceira.

9 Banco Princesa Alice

It's worth making the 50-nautical-mile (97-km) voyage out of Madalena on Pico to reach this dive spot celebrated for pelagic species such as the Chilean devil ray **(below)** and Galapagos shark.

10 Banco Dollabarat

Sited 20 nautical miles (37 km) to the northeast of Santa Maria and 3 nautical miles (5 km) from the Ilhéus das Formigas, this reserve is frequented by manta rays and sharks.

NEED TO KNOW

Parque Arqueológico Subaquático da Baía de Angra do Heroísmo: **MAP M6;** Angra do Heroísmo, Terceira; (295) 240 800

■ Visit dive.visitazores. com for more information about the islands' diving sites and centres.

■ The best time to dive in the Azores is from June to September.

■ Parque Arqueológico Subaquático da Baía de Angra do Heroísmo is an underwater archaeological park that features a number of shipwrecks and abandoned anchors.

Horta

Vibrant Horta on Faial is the yachting capital of the Azores, having served as an anchorage for caravels, clippers and seaplanes for hundreds of years. The late 19th century saw the installation of the first transatlantic cable stations, and today the town's cultural heritage draws on this link between the land and the sea. Museums bear testimony to the island's former whaling industry, while the mild climate helps parks and gardens flourish.

1 Casa dos Dabney
Out of Boston, the Dabney family settled on Faial in 1804. The cellar of their summer house is now home to a poignant exhibition that chronicles three early generations of the family *(see p38)*.

2 Casa-Museu Manuel de Arriaga
Manuel de Arriaga *(see p37)*, first president of the Republic of Portugal, was elected in 1911. His Horta home has been converted into a museum that celebrates the life of this political intellectual.

3 Jardim Botânico do Faial
Shrubs such as *Myrica faya* (after which Faial was named), Azores buckthorn and Azorean laurel are three of the endemic plants showcased in this public garden *(see p94)*.

4 Marina da Horta
Horta's popular marina **(above)** has berths for 300 yachts, and welcomes nearly 1,500 boats each year. Visiting crews leave their colourful calling cards on the harbour pier and walls – the largest maritime painting collection in the world.

5 Museu de Scrimshaw
The spear-like tusk of a narwhal, an Arctic whale dubbed the unicorn of the sea, is one of the more unusual exhibits **(left)** at this well-known museum. The exhibition of scrimshaw *(see p60)* is among the most comprehensive anywhere *(see p39)*.

6 Museu da Horta
A salon in this museum is dedicated to the fig tree pith sculptures **(left)** of Faial-born Euclides da Silveira Rosa (1910–1979). The museum also displays other eclectic exhibits *(see p38)*.

⑧ Fábrica da Baleia de Porto Pim

In its heyday this former factory was one of the most productive whaling stations in the Azores. An exhibition **(left)** and the engrossing interpretation centre tell its story.

Map of Horta

⑩ Miradouro do Monte da Guia

Sited near a chapel, this viewpoint is 100 m (328 ft) above sea level. The lofty views focus on Porto Pim and Horta, while Pico dominates the horizon.

⑨ Igreja de São Salvador

This 17th-century church **(right)** is known for its gilded woodwork and chapels. The altar of the Holy Sacrament is fronted by an engraved silver antependium *(see p41)*.

⑦ Aquário de Porto Pim

Various fish species are reared for here before being rehoused in aquariums abroad *(see p90)*.

NEED TO KNOW

Casa dos Dabney: **MAP T4**; Complexo Monte da Guia; (292) 240 685; open Jun–Sep: 10am–6pm daily; Oct–May: 10am–5pm Tue–Fri, 2–5:30pm Sat; adm €3.50 (includes entry to Aquário do Porto Pim), under 12s free

Casa-Museu Manuel de Arriaga: **MAP S3**; Rua Monsenhor José de Freitas Fortuna; (292) 293 361; open Apr–Sep: 10am–5:30pm Tue–Sun; Oct–Mar: 9:30am–5pm Tue–Sun; adm €2 (free Sun), under 14s free

Jardim Botânico do Faial: **MAP J3**; Rua da São Lourenço 23; (292) 948 140; open 10am–6pm daily (Oct–May: to 5pm Tue–Sat); adm €3.50, under 12s free

Museu do Scrimshaw: **MAP T3**; Rua José Azevedo 9; adm €2.50, under 12s free; www.petercafesport.com

Museu da Horta & Igreja de São Salvador: **MAP T2**; Largo Duque D'Avila e Bolama; (292) 392 784; open Jun–Sep: 10am–5:30pm Tue–Sun; Oct–May: 9:30am–5pm Tue–Sun; adm €2 (free Sun), under 14s free

Aquário de Porto Pim: **MAP S4**; (292) 207 382; open Jun–Sep: 10am–5pm Tue–Sun; Oct–May: 10am–5pm Tue–Fri, 2–5:30pm Sat; adm €3.50 (includes entry to Casa dos Dabney), under 12s free

Fábrica da Baleia de Porto Pim: **MAP T4**; Monte da Guia; (292) 292 140; opening times vary (call for details); adm €3, under 12s free

▪ Dive with whale sharks at the Princesa Alice seamount *(see p25)*. Visit norbertodiver.pt for more details.

🔟 ⭐ Capelinhos

Thunderous earthquakes, volcanic eruptions, molten lava lakes and a cloud of muddy debris forever altered the social and geological fabric of Capelinhos, located in a quiet corner of western Faial. The explosive episodes of 1957–8 defined an era, but from the ashes rose one of the most coveted geosites in the Azores. Hikers should start below ground at the futuristic visitor centre before exploring this lunar-like landscape by heading to the top of the lighthouse, then traversing the volcano trail, basalt crunching underfoot.

1 Capelinhos Volcano

Located in the far west of Faial, this is one of the Azores' greatest attractions **(above)**. Earthquakes and submarine eruptions in 1957–8 added an area of around 2.5 sq km (1 sq mile) to the landmass *(see p42)*.

THE CAPELINHOS ERUPTION

The tremors that began on 16 September 1957 heralded a continuous period of volcanic and seismic activity around Capelinhos. The boiling sea and hissing vapour developed into violent explosions. By mid-March 1958 a new island was attached to the mainland by a cord of steaming black ash. The Capelinhos eruption was a seminal event that destroyed 300 houses and made 2,000 people homeless.

2 Formação do Arquipélago dos Açores

The thousands of years it took to form the present-day Azores is condensed into an engaging 3D film shown at the Capelinhos interpretative centre. It houses an exhibition hall that displays a sample of volcanic rock collected from each island.

3 Sala Holograma

Inside the interpretative centre is the Hologram Hall where holographic animation re-creates the 13 months of submarine and subaerial tremors and eruptions before the final seismic blast.

4 Farol dos Capelinhos

The highlight for many is the climb to the top of the now-abandoned lighthouse **(below)**, the only building that withstood the eruptions.

5 Parque Florestal do Capelo

The Capelo Recreational Forest Reserve *(see p94)* offers a leafy alternative to the stark, barren Capelinhos environment. A protected area, the park is noted for its endemic flora, in particular an abundance of laurel.

6 Ten Volcanoes Trail

The ascent from the interpretative centre leads hikers through the fertile lowlands of Capelo before climbing towards Faial's immense *caldeira*, following an alignment of some of the island's oldest volcanic cones along the way *(see p47)*.

7 Protected Landscape

The unique lunar-like landscape created in the wake of the eruption, considered one of the most definitive volcanic events of recent years, is classified as a protected nature reserve of geological, biological and aesthetic interest.

8 Centro de Interpretação do Vulcão dos Capelinhos

This underground interpretative centre **(above)** provides plenty of information about the Capelinhos eruption and volcanology *(see p91)*.

9 Capelo–Capelinhos Trail

A walk of moderate difficulty, the trail begins at the Cabeço Verde volcanic cone in the Capelo Recreational Forest Reserve. The 55-m (180-ft) deep Furna Ruim lava cave en route is a photographic highlight.

10 Caldeira

Encircled by an emerald mantle of native vegetation splashed with lilac-hued hydrangeas, the island's crater **(below)** offers a broad, inspirational prospect over the Capelinhos peninsula *(see p91)*.

NEED TO KNOW

Centro de Interpretação do Vulcão dos Capelinhos: **MAP G2**; Capelinhos; (292) 200 470; open Jun–Sep: 10am–6pm daily; Oct–May: 10am–5pm Tue–Fri, 2–5:30pm Sat & Sun; guided tours from 11am daily (call ahead for timings); adm €10, 13–17-year-olds & over 65s €5, under 12s free; parquesnaturais. azores.gov.pt

■ There is a café-bar in the foyer of the interpretative centre.

■ The Roadman's House (Estrada da Caldeira; (292) 207 382; open 10am–5pm Mon–Fri) works as an interpretative centre where the geology, flora and fauna of the Reserva Natural do Caldeira do Faial is explained, and walking trails and viewpoints are outlined.

■ Visitors can also explore Casa dos Botes (Porto do Comprido; open Jun–Sep: 10am–1pm & 2–6pm daily) in Capelinhos, a former whalers' boathouse recovered from the ashes of the volcanic eruption and subsequently rebuilt. It serves as a reminder of Faial's once flourishing whaling industry.

TOP 10 ⭐ Algar do Carvão

In the heart of Terceira, the Algar do Carvão cave system is a compelling subterranean spectacle. Formed two millennia ago during the dying days of a fiery volcano, this huge lava tube appears as though blasted from the island's core, its walls and ceiling bearing the scars of a fierce meltdown. Entering this underworld of stalactites and stalagmites is to tread the dark recesses of the earth, where nature is the architect of some extraordinary chambers and caverns. Deeper still, a pit cradles a lake. Linger in this ethereal hollow and reflect on the powerful forces that created it.

1 Bola Gasosa
A striking geological anomaly greeting visitors as they enter the first chamber is the "gaseous ball" – the walled imprint of a huge basaltic gas bubble **(right)**. Its shape resembles the wide-open eye of a giant.

3 Caldeira de Guilherme Moniz
Algar do Carvão is located near Terceira's central crater, the 15-km (9-mile) perimeter of which places it among the largest in the Azores. The region falls within the boundaries of a natural reserve, an area of Macaronesian scrubland and peat bogs **(left)**.

4 Lagoa
Set 80 m (262 ft) within the belly of the cave is a lake. Nourished by rainfall, this hidden lagoon is normally around 15 m (50 ft) deep but dries up almost completely in summer due to low precipitation.

5 Stalactites
The world's largest concentration of amorphous silica stalactites **(below)** is found here. Up to 1 m (3 ft) long, these rare milky-white structures ornament large areas of the ceiling.

2 Boca do Algar do Carvão
The mouth of the cave bristles with endemic flora – a treat for botanists and speleologists. There are 34 species of liverwort and 22 varieties of moss.

NEED TO KNOW

MAP M5 ▪ Algar do Carvão ▪ (295) 212 992

Open Apr & May: 3–5:30pm daily; Jun & Sep: 2:30–5:45pm daily; Jul & Aug: 2–6pm daily; Oct–Mar: 3–5pm Mon, Wed & Fri

Adm €6, under 12s free

▪ The Associação Os Montanheiros (Rua da Rocha 8, Angra do Heroísmo; (295) 212 992; www.montanheiros.com) is an association of speleologists that facilitates access to the vast network of caves spread across the archipelago (see p80).

Visitors inside Algar do Carvão cave

A 2,000-YEAR-OLD NATURAL WONDER

Algar do Carvão is a huge lava tube around 100 m (328 ft) in length, a cavern in a basalt scoria cone formed during a volcanic eruption some 2,000 years ago. The outer chamber can be accessed via a vertical vent that drops 45 m (147 ft) from the mouth of the cave. A second conduit falls to an inner cave, the base of which is filled by a lake, situated 80 m (262 ft) from the uppermost reaches of the tube. The cave is classified as a Regional Natural Monument.

⑦ Cave-Dwelling Spider

Sharp-eyed cavers might chance upon the elusive *Turinyphia cavernicola*, an endemic spider found only in Algar do Carvão. The webs of these cave-dwelling arachnids can be spotted between the ancient fissures.

⑧ Other Troglobitic Insects

Perfectly adapted to the underground life is *Trechus terceiranus*, a copper-coloured beetle endemic to Terceira. Another Algar resident that will interest entomologists is *Lithobius obscuras azorae*, a species of centipede.

⑨ The "Cathedral"

Of massive proportions, the cavern's inner chamber draws gasps for its imposing domed roof streaked with glassy obsidian. The vault's pure acoustics mean it is often the stage for subterranean music concerts.

⑥ Ferns and Other Flora

The underside of the cave entrance is radiant enough to sustain ferns, their delicate emerald fronds backlit by the sparse sunlight. Green algae and mould can be spotted in the cave's deeper recesses.

⑩ Furnas do Enxofre

Sulphurous fumaroles **(below)** near the Algar cave complex bubble up from the tangled undergrowth over which a purpose-built footpath snakes and dips.

TOP 10 ⭐ Paisagem da Cultura da Vinha da Ilha do Pico

The UNESCO-protected "Landscape of Pico Island Vineyard Culture" is made up of coastal vineyards, corralled into pockets by basalt walls. Here, the island's winemaking tradition is evident in the distilleries, cellars and warehouses in hamlets where *adegas* (wineries) have been producing wine for centuries. Plan a visit during harvest, which is celebrated with song and dance, and when festivals pair the best wines with home-style food.

1 Museu do Vinho

A former Carmelite convent building houses the wine museum. The grounds can be seen from a viewing platform set over the *currais* (double walls) and *curraletas* (basalt-walled plots) that enclose the vines *(see p38).*

2 Rilheiras

Numerous lava slabs **(left)** have been moulded by *rilheiras* (wheel tracks) of carts laden with goods hauled by oxen, once the only effective method of transportation. Many are found near the coast.

3 Cooperativa Vitivinícola

A guided visit to this long-established wine cooperative finishes with a tasting of the island's best-known wines. Prominent labels include Basalto and Terras de Lava *(see p93).*

NEED TO KNOW

Museu do Vinho: **MAP L2;** Rua do Carmo, near Madalena; (292) 622 147; open summer: 10am–5:30pm Tue–Sun, winter: 9:30am–5pm Tue–Sun; adm €2 (free Sun), 14–25-year-olds & over 65s €1, under 13s free

Centro de Interpretação da Paisagem da Cultura da Vinha da Ilha do Pico: **MAP M2;** Lajido; open Jun–Sep: 10am–6pm daily; Oct–May: 10am–5pm Tue–Fri, 1:30–5pm Sat & Sun; adm €2, concessions, under 12s free; guided tour of the centre: €7, concessions, under 12s free

■ On most days, women in traditional costume can be found on the Moinho do Frode verandah selling local handicrafts.

■ Free organized tours of Pico's Santa Luzia-Lajido vineyards take place at 10:30am every Friday. Call (962) 576 101 for details.

④ Rola-Pipas

Scout the water's edge and spot the smooth telltale ramps that are hollowed out of serrated basalt. These facilitated the movement of wine barrels to the nearest port. They are called *rola-pipas*, and it was no easy task levelling out the stubborn terrain this way.

Pico's vineyards enclosed by basalt walls

⑨ Centro de Interpretação da Paisagem da Cultura da Vinha da Ilha do Pico

This interpretative centre **(above)** explains Pico's viniculture and highlights the wines produced here. A visit to a traditional distillery is included, and there's an opportunity to taste the wines.

VINES, VINEYARDS AND WINE

Popular lore suggests that the parish priest of Lajes was the first to plant vines on Pico in the late 15th century. The mid-1500s saw the advent of Pico's viniculture but stony, lava-strewn soil and salt-laced squalls made cultivation arduous. The solution was to build *currais* from the loose volcanic debris to shield the vines from winds and sea spray, and to retain the daytime heat. These plots or *curraletas* characterize Pico's vineyard landscape.

---

⑤ Santana–Lajido Trail

Beginning in Santana village, this trail takes visitors past the Baía do Gasparal and its former cargo dock. There are fine examples of *rola-pipas* here. The route skirts the coast to Lajido, a hamlet known for its fig-distilled firewater.

⑦ Vinhas da Criação Velha Trail

This walk offers stunning views of Pico and Faial mountains, skirting the vineyards and passing the harbour, ending at Porto do Calhau. Look out for the rare *vidalii (see p53)* with its bell-shaped blooms **(left)**.

⑩ Moinho do Frade

The iconic cylindrical windmill with its red bonnet **(below)** looms over the noted Criação Velha vineyards that lie west of Madalena. Once used to mill grain, the carefully restored landmark offers a wonderful view across the vicinity.

⑥ Tidal Wells

These box-shaped wells were built to capture fresh water running underground to the sea, the accumulation of which was influenced by tidal currents.

⑧ Alambique

Still in use today, the *alambique* (distillery) in Lajido located opposite the interpretative centre produces *aguardente de figo e de vinho*, a grape- and fig-concoction.

The Top 10 of Everything

Altar of Igreja Matriz de São Sebastião
in Ponta Delgada, São Miguel

🔟 Moments in History

1 Discovery
The first map to depict the Azores was the 1351 *Medici Atlas*, which outlined the seven islands of the Central and Eastern Groups. It is debated who rediscovered the Azores. The first island spotted by Portuguese explorers, between 1427 and 1432, was Santa Maria. Flores and Corvo, in the Western Group, were not discovered until 1452.

Christopher Columbus

2 Settlement
By the mid-15th century Portuguese and Flemish explorers had visited the archipelago. Named *Açores* by early settlers after they supposedly sighted goshawks *(see p52)*, the first islands to be populated were Santa Maria and São Miguel, followed by Terceira and Graciosa in 1450. By 1466 settlements had appeared on São Jorge, Faial and Pico. Flores was colonized around 1504, while Corvo saw the first semblance of a community by 1548.

3 Christopher Columbus
In 1493 Christopher Columbus made a stop just off the fishing village of Anjos, Santa Maria while on his return from the Americas. It is believed that a small crew rowed ashore to offer prayers for their safe haven at the tiny Capela de Nossa Senhora dos Anjos *(see p41)*.

4 Commercial Development
By the mid-16th century the islands provided anchorage for vessels returning from India. Brazil's colonization by Portugal and America's discovery also led to development of infrastructure across Azores, especially Angra do Heroísmo.

5 Conquest of the Azores
In 1583 Spanish troops, led by Álvaro de Bazán, clashed with islanders and French and English soldiers on Terceira. Overwhelmed by the Spanish army's superior numbers, the defence crumbled. Terceira and the Kingdom of Portugal were taken over by Filipe II (1521–1598). In 1640 the Portuguese monarchy was restored and the Azores liberated.

6 Liberals and Absolutists
Portugal's 1820 Liberal revolution reverberated across the Azores. The Absolutists targeted Terceira, the last Liberal stronghold,

A 16th-century painting depicting the conquest of the Azores

and in 1829 attempted unsuccessfully to land at Vila da Praia. Following their defeat, it was renamed Praia da Vitória *(see p78)*. Angra became the capital of Portugal until 1833. It was later named Angra do Heroísmo.

7 World War II

The archipelago's strategic value increased after the US entered World War II. Lajes Field was built on Terceira in 1943, an air base from which Allied forces fought German U-boats. Today, Lajes remains a US-Portuguese military base, contributing towards NATO's strategic role and supervising commercial air traffic.

A fighter jet at present-day Lajes Field

8 The Capelinhos Eruption

A series of earth tremors that began on 16 September 1957 led to an underwater volcanic eruption on 27 September off the Faial coast, near Capelinhos. Explosions in early 1958 formed a new landmass, destroyed many houses and left 2,000 people homeless *(see pp28–9)*.

9 Autonomy

In 1976 the Azores became an autonomous region of Portugal, with its own government. However, Lisbon still controls education, health, and the army, police and judiciary. The Azores' president resides in Ponta Delgada.

10 Whaling Ban

Portugal's ratification of the Berne Convention on the Conservation of European Wildlife and Natural Habitats in 1982 banned whale hunting in the Azores. Today, it is among the world's best whale-watching destinations *(see pp16–17)*.

TOP 10 HISTORIC FIGURES

Manuel de Arriaga

1 Thomas Hickling (1745–1834)
American merchant who built a summer residence in gardens that later became the Parque Terra Nostra *(see p18)*.

2 John Bass Dabney (1766–1826)
Patriarch of the Dabney family and first US consul to the Azores *(see p26)*.

3 António José Severim de Noronha (1792–1860)
Count of Vila Flor, Noronha commanded the Liberal armies and secured victory against the Absolutists at Vila da Praia.

4 Carlos Machado (1828–1901)
An eminent naturalist, Machado created the Azorean Museum in 1876. Renamed in his honour, the museum was rehoused in a convent in 1930 *(see p39)*.

5 Manuel de Arriaga (1840–1917)
The first elected President of the Republic of Portugal was born in Horta. A museum celebrates his life *(see p26)*.

6 Prince Albert I of Monaco (1848–1922)
The royal explorer visited the Azores several times, and made the first descent of Furna do Enxofre *(see p42)*.

7 Francisco de Lacerda (1869–1934)
Composer noted for his affinity for traditional Azorean music. A museum houses personal artifacts *(see p92)*.

8 Ernesto Canto da Maia (1890–1981)
Sculptor and vanguard of Portuguese Modernist art. His work is on display at the Museu Carlos Machado's Núcleo de Santa Bárbara *(see p39)*.

9 Domingos Rebelo (1891–1975)
Rebelo is revered for paintings such as *Os Imigrantes* (The Emigrants).

10 Natália Correia (1923–1993)
A poet and social activist, Correia wrote the lyrics of the *Hino dos Açores* (Hymn of the Azores), the regional anthem.

🔟 Museums

Viewing pavilion at the Museu do Vinho set over Pico's iconic vineyards

1 Museu do Vinho
Pico's wine and vineyard culture is explained at this engaging museum. Set within an old Carmelite convent, the main building overlooks a UNESCO-protected landscape of vines. An annexe houses a vintage winepress. Visitors can taste and buy Pico wines here *(see p32)*.

2 Museu de Angra do Heroísmo
Curated with considerable flair and imagination, the permanent exhibition "From the Sea and Land... a Story in the Atlantic" traces Terceira's evolution, from its discovery in the 15th century to 19th-century industrialization. The museum is housed in the old Convento de São Francisco, and the convent's splendid church interior is a rewarding detour *(see p20)*.

An astrolabe at Museu de Angra do Heroísmo

3 Museu da Horta
A former Jesuit college is home to an exhibition that illustrates the island's history. Highlights include a section dedicated to Horta's 19th-century cable-telegraph stations and vintage bronze diving helmets. Do not miss the collection of fig tree pith sculptures *(see p61)*, the largest of its kind in the world *(see p26)*.

4 Casa dos Dabney
Three generations of Dabneys, a family from Boston, are chronicled at this museum-house. Influential in Horta business and social circles, the Dabneys established shipping and whaling enterprises, and also served as US consuls. The complex includes the Aquário de Porto Pim *(see p27)*.

5 Núcleo de Arte Sacra – Igreja do Colégio
The sacred art collection from the Museu Carlos Machado is exhibited here. There are paintings, sculpture and silverware, plus 17th- and 18th-century Indo-Portuguese ivory religious figurines. But it is the church's altarpiece and tiled panels that astound *(see p13)*.

6 Museu das Flores
This ethnographic museum explores the heritage of the island and its inhabitants' relationship with the land and the sea. The collection is displayed around an internal cloister of the enchanting Baroque Convento de São Boaventura *(see p100)*.

7 Museu de Scrimshaw
The world's largest private collection of scrimshaw is on view in a room above the well-known Peter

Café Sport *(see p96)*. Besides the remarkable engravings on whales' teeth, there are canes, cutlery, picture frames, needle boxes and other items shaped from whalebone *(see p26)*.

8 Museu Carlos Machado

MAP V1 ▪ Rua Dr Carlos Machado, Ponta Delgada, São Miguel ▪ (296) 202 930 ▪ Open Apr–Sep: 10am–5:30pm Tue–Sun; Oct–Mar: 9:30am–5pm Tue–Sun ▪ Adm ▪ museucarlosmachado.azores.gov.pt

Centered around two permanent exhibitions, the Natural History and Convent Memory collections, this outstanding museum is housed in the 16th-century Convento de Santo André. The bird hall contains fine examples of the taxidermist's art and species include the now-extinct Carolina parakeet *(see p13)*.

Sta Teresinha, **Museu dos Baleeiros**

9 Museu dos Baleeiros

The Whalers' Museum provides a fascinating insight into whaling in the Azores until 1985. The exhibition is set within three original 19th-century boathouses and displayed around the *Sta. Teresinha*, a restored traditional whaling boat. Exhibits include tools, handcrafted harpoons and fine examples of scrimshaw *(see p91)*.

10 Museu da Graciosa

A contemporary wing provides a dramatic contrast against the original museum, housed in a late 19th-century building. Traditional farming tools, costumes, earthenware, an old winepress and period furniture form the exhibition. Look out for the annexed Barracão de Canoas, an old whaler's boathouse *(see p81)*.

TOP 10 RARE OR UNUSUAL EXHIBITS IN AZOREAN MUSEUMS

1 Núcleo de Arte Sacra – Igreja do Colégio
The two paintings of the *Coroação da Virgem* (Coronation of the Virgin) by Vasco Pereira Lusitano (1533–1608).

2 Museu Carlos Machado
The Cedro do Mato, a 4,000-year-old cedar wood branch found on a mountain during construction of the Sete Cidades tunnel in the 1930s.

3 Museu de Angra do Heroísmo
The 1893-built "Paper Boat", a wooden-ribbed vessel, lined with layers of glued newspaper and coated with canvas.

4 Museu da Graciosa
Figurehead, probably representing Venus, carved from a single block of pine wood (c.1850–1900), salvaged from the schooner *Julia*.

5 Museu dos Baleeiros
Beautifully carved and engraved nautilus conch shell, illustrated with pastoral scenes.

6 Museu do Vinho
The "Aroma" game. Activate an aroma from a cylinder and match it to various fruits, vegetables and condiments.

7 Museu da Horta
The headstone from the grave of the first settler and captain-major of Faial, Josse van Huerter (1430–95).

8 Museu de Scrimshaw
A solid lump of ambergris, produced in the digestive system of sperm whales. Highly sought after for its use in making perfumes.

9 Casa dos Dabney
The diary of Rose Dabney Forbes (1864–1947), an illuminated manuscript and a calligraphic triumph. Only 15 copies of it were printed.

10 Museu das Flores
An early 20th-century folding marine chair created entirely out of the jawbone of a sperm whale.

Figurehead, Museu da Graciosa

🔟 Churches and Chapels

Altarpiece of Igreja do Colégio

17th century, the church is a picture of sculptured harmony and its façade brims with twirling flourishes of lava stone embellished with floral motifs.

③ Igreja de Santa Bárbara

Nestled amongst gardens overlooking the sea, the idyllic location is reason enough to visit this beautiful church. But the real eye-opener is its gilded Baroque interior. The focus is a richly carved retable and the polished panels of *azulejos* (tiles) illustrating the story of Santa Bárbara *(see p89)*.

④ Igreja da Misericórdia

MAP V4 ■ Pátio da Alfândega, Angra do Heroísmo, Terceira ■ Adm

One of the Azores' most recognized religious buildings, this 18th-century church stands on the site of a hospital, built in 1492 and the first in the Azores. A guided tour highlights the church's rich patrimony, marvellous acoustic qualities and the damage caused by the 1980 earthquake *(see p79)*. Ask to see the catacombs, not always included in the tour *(see p20)*.

⑤ Igreja de São Boaventura

MAP R5 ■ Rua do Hospital, Santa Cruz das Flores, Flores ■ Adm

The mustard-coloured façade is a landmark, and it is worth exploring the interior of this 17th-century

① Igreja do Colégio

An exuberant façade hints at the rich interior of this early-17th-century church. A carved altarpiece of majestic proportions, dazzling in its Baroque ornamentation, remains partially gilded after the Jesuits were expelled in 1759. Colourful tiled panels under a triumphal arch depict Eucharistic allegories *(see p12)*.

② Igreja de Nossa Senhora da Purificação

MAP F2 ■ Santo Espírito, Santa Maria

According to local legend, this 16th-century church is linked to the first Holy Spirit festivals *(see p62)* in the Azores. Enlarged in the

Igreja de Nossa Senhora da Purificação

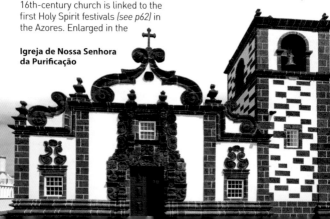

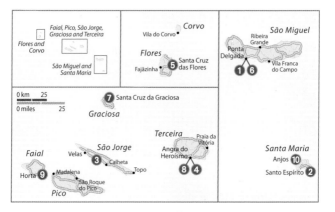

building. An extension of the Baroque Convento de São Boaventura, now a museum (see p38), the church's highlight is the vaulted cedarwood ceiling festooned with botanical motifs and allegorical figures.

6 Convento e Santuário de Nossa Senhora da Esperança

The santuário (sanctuary) of the Convent of Our Lady of Hope displays the Ecce Homo figure, adorned with a quintet of sacred art representing *Glory*, *Crown*, *Sceptre*, *Cords* and *Reliquary*. The standout piece is *Glory*, crafted from gold-plated platinum and encrusted with 6,842 precious stones. The ritual of Senhor Santo Cristo dos Milagres (see p62) has close associations with this 16th-century statue (see p13).

Wooden figurine of Ecce Homo

7 Ermida da Nossa Senhora da Ajuda

MAP K5 ■ Santa Cruz da Graciosa, Graciosa ■ Closed to the public

Crowning the Monte da Ajuda (see p81) summit, this 16th-century fortress-style building has a façade of plastered masonry, chunky buttresses, cornices, frames and decorative elements in exposed basalt. A finger-like belfry gives it a lopsided perspective.

8 Convento de São Gonçalo

MAP U4 ■ Rua Gonçalo V. Cabral, Angra do Heroísmo, Terceira ■ Open 10am–5:30pm Mon–Fri ■ Adm

Founded in 1545, the convent is the oldest in Angra do Heroísmo and the largest in the Azores. The church is noted for its outstanding figured choir decorated in gilded wood. The filigree crucifix in the chancel is a splendid example of 17th-century silverwork (see p20).

9 Igreja de São Salvador

The late-17th-century São Salvador church was originally part of a Jesuit college, which functioned until the Jesuits were expelled from Portugal in 1759. Gilded chapels and tiled panels embellish the interior (see p27).

10 Capela de Nossa Senhora dos Anjos

Anjos was Christopher Columbus' first landfall on his return from the Americas in 1493. Some of his crew are said to have offered prayers here. The chapel's triptych is believed to have originated from the caravel of Portuguese explorer Gonçalo Velho Cabral (see p69), credited with rediscovering Santa Maria between 1427 and 1432 (see p72).

🔟 Natural Wonders

1 Montanha do Pico

At 2,351 m (7,708 ft) Pico is the highest mountain in Portugal. The majestic sweep of this dormant stratovolcano's conical outline is one of the archipelago's most iconic symbols. Capping the pit crater at the top is a volcanic cone, which forms the mountain's summit (see pp88–9).

The rugged landscape of Capelinhos

2 Capelinhos

Bleak and austere, Capelinhos on Faial still bears the scars from a series of powerful earthquakes and volcanic eruptions that took place in 1957–8. The well-documented calamity reshaped the island and is regarded as a seminal volcanic event. Today the lunar-style landscape, replete with a lighthouse and a superb interpretative centre, is an evocative landmark (see pp28–9).

3 Algar do Carvão

The largest concentration of amorphous silica stalactites in the world can be found deep within this volcanic cave system. The mesmerizing interior is reached by descending a near-vertical 45-m (147-ft) vent. At the bottom of the 80-m (262-ft) lava tube is a lake fed by rainwater (see pp30–31).

4 Lagoa das Furnas

Set in the picturesque Vale das Furnas, São Miguel's second-largest crater lake is surrounded by elevated forest-covered slopes. On the northern shore are hot water springs or fumaroles, known locally as *caldeiras*. The traditional *cozido das Furnas* is cooked by locals in the hot earth here (see p19).

5 Furna do Enxofre

Graciosa's impressive caldera includes the Furna do Enxofre cave. The cavern features a huge domed ceiling – a rare volcanic phenomenon. The floor is reached by descending a concrete spiral staircase. A wide lake occupies the deepest recesses of the cave. Graciosa itself is a UNESCO Biosphere Reserve (see p78).

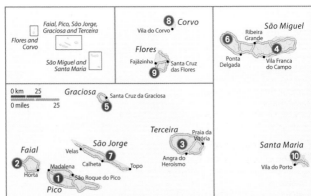

Faial, Pico, São Jorge, Graciosa and Terceira

Flores and Corvo

São Miguel and Santa Maria

0 km — 25
0 miles — 25

8 Corvo
Vila do Corvo •

Flores
Fajãzinha • • Santa Cruz
das Flores
9

Graciosa • Santa Cruz da Graciosa
5

São Miguel
Ribeira Grande
6 •
Ponta Delgada • • Vila Franca do Campo
4

Terceira Praia da Vitória
3
Angra do Heroísmo

Faial
Horta
2 • Velas • *São Jorge*
Madalena Calheta • • Topo
7
São Roque do Pico
1
Pico

Santa Maria
Vila do Porto •
10

The picturesque Lagoa das Sete Cidades surrounded by lush greenery

⑥ Lagoa das Sete Cidades

Sunk within the verdant perimeter of an ancient caldera, the twin lakes – Lagoa Verde and Lagoa Azul (the Green Lake and the Blue Lake) – have a compelling charm. The Vista do Rei viewpoint overlooks the dramatic landscape *(see pp14–15)*.

⑦ Fajã dos Cubres

Recognized by UNESCO as biosphere reserves, the island's *fajãs* (coastal plains created from lava flows or collapsing cliffs) are areas of outstanding natural beauty. One of the most celebrated is Fajã dos Cubres on the northern coast. A lagoon serves as a rich wetland habitat for a fascinating and diverse range of flora and fauna *(see p89)*.

⑧ Caldeirão

Twin lakes dotted with tiny islets enhance the romantic character of this crater, a 300-m (984-ft) deep caldera with a 2-km (1-mile) diameter. Singular in its appeal, the remoteness of Corvo – a UNESCO Biosphere Reserve – only adds to the crater's mystique *(see p100)*.

⑨ Rocha dos Bordões

Rising from a weathered escarpment, this curious-looking rock formation with huge vertical basalt columns resembles a prehistoric pipe organ and is a standout geological feature of the island, which is a UNESCO Biopshere Reserve. The solidified folds appear to change colour with the sun's trajectory *(see p101)*.

⑩ Deserto Vermelho dos Açores

An amazing anomaly known locally as Barreiro da Faneca, the "Red Desert of the Azores" is an undulating arid landscape of rust-coloured clayish soil that blankets an age-old basaltic lava flow. The oxidized terrain is unlike any other found in the archipelago and the entire region is a protected geosite *(see p69)*.

Deserto Vermelho dos Açores

TOP 10 Natural Swimming Pools and Thermal Springs

Caldeira Velha's mineral-rich waterfall

1 Caldeira Velha
MAP D5 ▪ Nr Ribeira Grande, São Miguel

Tucked away on the northern slopes of Lagoa do Fogo (see p68) is this idyllic bathing spot. A warm-water waterfall, rich in minerals, runs between lichen- and moss-coated boulders into a pond under a canopy of royal fern. There are changing rooms and picnic tables on site.

2 Biscoitos
Carved out of jagged, age-old basalt, the shallow pools at Biscoitos are among the most beautiful on Terceira. Float in calm, crystalline waters and revel in the spray as a wayward Atlantic roller thunders into the rocks creating an instant salt-laced shower (see p78).

3 Ponta da Ferraria
MAP A5 ▪ São Miguel ▪ Spa: adm ▪ www.termasferraria.com

A natural swimming pool formed of solidified lava, the salt water is heated by a bubbling spring. Crashing waves cool it enough for a relaxing dip. The neighbouring spa offers a more sophisticated wellbeing experience.

4 Poça da Dona Beija
This thermal spring complex has five Jacuzzi-like bathing areas, each one fed by the warm waters Furnas is famous for. Changing rooms, hot and cold showers, and lockers are among the amenities. Arrive after dark and the whole place is fantastically illuminated (see p19).

5 Santa Cruz das Flores
MAP R5 ▪ Flores

Knee-deep in places when the tide is out, the water here is comfortably warm in summer. A basalt ridge tames the surf so it pours gently into the pools. A short stroll from Santa Cruz town centre, this is a prime sunbathing spot for locals.

6 Criação Velha
MAP L2 ▪ Nr Madalena, Pico

When swimming here on a sunny morning, Faial, across the channel, looks close enough to touch. This collection of green pools is protected from the restless sway of the Atlantic waves by craggy black lava clusters.

Natural pool at Biscoitos

7 Calheta

Kids will enjoy the water slide built over the edge of this attractive natural pool at Calheta *(see p92)*. On cloudless days the dramatic cone of Montanha do Pico *(see p42)* is clearly visible.

Enjoying a soak at Piscina de Água

8 Piscina de Água – Parque Terra Nostra

The muddy water should not deter visitors: the thermal spring supplying the pool contains essential minerals, flowing in at 35–40° C (95–104° F) temperature. Surrounded by botanical gardens, this iron-rich oasis works wonders on tired muscles *(see p18)*.

9 Varadouro

MAP H2 ▪ Nr Ribeira do Cabo, Faial

This wide, irregular-shaped pool is enclosed but for a half-submerged tunnel bored into the wall, designed to channel the ocean's swell. An adjacent toddlers' pool makes Varadouro ideal for families.

10 Carapacho

Ideal for snorkelling, the natural rock pools here are partly enclosed by a concrete breakwater. A bonus is the annexed swimming pool heated by the therapeutic waters from the nearby Carapacho Spa, renowned for its treatments for skin disorders and rheumatism *(see p79)*.

TOP 10 BEACHES

1 Praia de Água d'Alto
MAP D6 ▪ Nr Vila Franco do Campo, São Miguel
A wide swathe of sand overlooked by hotel Pestana Bahia Praia *(see p113)*.

2 Praia de Santa Bárbara
MAP C5 ▪ Ribeira Grande, São Miguel
A long boardwalk serves this sizeable beach preferred by surfers. Amenities include a pool complex and a restaurant.

3 Praia do Pópulo
MAP C6 ▪ Nr Lagoa, São Miguel
East of Ponta Delgada *(see pp12–13)*, this "popular" beach lives up to its name.

4 Praia da Formosa
MAP E2 ▪ Santa Maria
Formosa is endowed with a band of soft white sand, rare in the Azores.

5 Praia de Angra do Heroísmo
MAP U4 ▪ Terceira
A city beach upgraded and expanded, this slither of sand is a family favourite.

6 Praia da Vitória
MAP P5 ▪ Terceira
The marina and sweeping promenade lend this place a resort-like ambience.

7 Praia
MAP K5 ▪ Graciosa
Praia's light sandy beach is wrapped around a sheltered bay.

8 Praia do Almoxarife
MAP K3 ▪ Nr Facho, Faial
This picturesque black-sand half-moon beach is a high-season hit.

9 Praia do Porto Pim
MAP T4 ▪ Faial
Close to Horta's town centre, the beach lies under Monte da Guia *(see p27)*.

10 Praia Fajã Grande
MAP Q6 ▪ Flores
Secluded beach set against a splendid backdrop of cascading waterfalls.

The sweep of Praia do Porto Pim

🔟 Walks and Hikes

A trail leading to the viewpoint that gives a sweeping view of Sete Cidades

1 Lagoa do Canário–Sete Cidades–Mosteiros

MAP B5–A4 ▪ São Miguel

The 14-km (9-mile) walk begins at Lagoa do Canário in Carvão. Marvel at the panorama from Miradouro da Grota do Inferno and then stroll along the northeastern rim of Caldeira das Sete Cidades *(see pp14–15)*. The route descends into Mosteiros on the coast.

2 Serra Branca–Praia

MAP J6–K5 ▪ Graciosa

A picturesque amble, the trail begins in Serra Branca, crossing the island from west to east. Gentle on the legs, the 7-km (4-mile) trek will take around 2 hours, more if walkers go around the rim of the caldera *(see p78)*.

3 Montanha do Pico

The ascent of Pico *(see pp88–9)* is an ambition of many hikers visiting the Azores. Reaching the summit of Portugal's highest mountain is

The summit of Montanha do Pico

rewarded with stunning views of the surrounding islands. The trail begins at Cabeço das Cabras reception centre 1,200 m (4,000 ft) up the mountain.

4 Vila do Porto–Baía da Praia

MAP E2 ▪ Santa Maria

The 16th-century Forte de Sao Brás *(see p72)* marks the starting point of a moderate 3-hour, 11-km (7-mile) walk that skirts the coast towards Praia da Formosa. Landmarks include the volcanic hillock of Facho de Vila and Fonte do Mourato village.

5 Serreta–Ponta do Raminho

MAP L5–4 ▪ Terceira

From Serreta village *(see p80)* and following a well-trodden path through a bucolic landscape, this 10-km (6-mile) circuit takes around 4 hours to complete. Explore Reserva Florestal de Recreio da Mata da Serreta en route.

6 Caldeirinhas–Norte Grande

MAP N1–P1 ▪ São Jorge

This route commences 700 m (2,300 ft) above sea level, so check the weather forecast beforehand. The 15-km (9-mile) trail along the spine of the island follows the central ridge to Pico da Esperança, the highest summit on São Jorge, before making a descent towards the coast. Admire breathtaking views along the way.

7 Caldeira–Capelinhos
MAP G2–H2 ■ Faial

Known as the *Trilho dos Dez Vulcões* (Ten Volcanoes Trail), this is an exhilarating 8-hour, 20-km (12-mile) hike. Occasionally difficult, the route snakes up from the Centro de Interpretação do Vulcão dos Capelinhos through impressive scenery towards the caldera *(see p29)*.

8 Lajedo–Fajã Grande–Ponta Delgada

Europe's westernmost hiking trail, the scenic 22-km (14-mile) course offers a stark contrast between the coast and countryside. It passes through geological wonders such as Rocha dos Bordões *(see p43)*. The distance can be covered in a day, but many choose to undertake the journey in two stages, or prefer to start their walk from Ponta Delgada *(see p99)*.

Walking track between fields on Pico

9 São Roque do Pico–Ladeira dos Moinhos
MAP N2 ■ Pico

A circular route of a little over 3 km (2 miles) beginning and ending in São Roque do Pico, this walk takes in a cobbled footpath and six watermills. The gentle incline reveals pleasant views of the town and the coast.

10 Vila do Corvo–Caldeirão
MAP R4 ■ Corvo

The smallest and most remote island of the archipelago is best explored on foot. This moderate 4-km (2-mile) jaunt takes hikers from the harbour at Vila do Corvo to the edge of the Caldeirão, which features two beautiful lakes.

TOP 10 IMPRESSIVE VIEWPOINTS

Miradouro Caldeira do Faial

1 Miradouro da Vista do Rei
MAP A5 ■ São Miguel
The main viewpoint of the island overlooks both lakes of Sete Cidades.

2 Miradouro de Santa Iria
MAP D5 ■ São Miguel
Excellent clifftop views are accompanied by calls of Cory's shearwaters *(see p53)*.

3 Miradouro da Macela
MAP E2 ■ Santa Maria
The outlook embraces Praia village, its white-sand beach and the bay beyond.

4 Miradouro do Raminho
MAP L4 ■ Terceira
Steep cliffs, headlands created from lava flows and the lighthouse, Farol da Serreta, are included in the panorama.

5 Miradouro do Pico Timão
MAP J5 ■ Graciosa
Admire the Serra Branca pastures from the island's second-highest point.

6 Miradouro da Fajã do Ouvidor
MAP P1 ■ São Jorge
On clear days inspiring sea views are enhanced by a glimpse of Graciosa.

7 Miradouro de São Miguel Arcanjo
MAP N3 ■ Pico
The quaint village of Prainha sits against a wild seascape.

8 Miradouro Caldeira do Faial
MAP H2 ■ Faial
Marvel at breathtaking views of a 400-m (1,300-ft) deep and 1,500-m (5,000-ft) wide crater from here.

9 Miradouro da Fajãzinha
MAP Q6 ■ Flores
This lookout offers a spectacular vista of the scenic Ribeira Grande valley.

10 Miradouro do Portal
MAP R4 ■ Corvo
Cup your hands and you seem to enclose Vila do Corvo from this perch.

Following pages A slipper lobster spotted in waters off the Santa Maria coast

Outdoor Activities

A bottlenose dolphin off Faial

1 Diving and Snorkelling
Arraia Divers: www.arraia divers.com

Crystalline waters, a rich marine ecosystem and a seabed of volcanic caves and tunnels make the Azores one of Europe's most fascinating diving destinations. Around 28 species of cetaceans, five types of sea turtles and over 600 fish species can be spotted in waters off the islands (see pp24–5).

2 Canoeing and Kayaking
Azores For All: azoresforall.com

Exploring the islands' crater lakes (see pp14–15) by canoe is a beguiling experience. Paddling silently under the rim of a volcano is an awe-inspiring activity. Out on the ocean, the communion with nature is equally palpable. Sea kayaking offers access to hidden grottoes, islets and stacks.

3 Whale Watching
Espaço Talassa: www.espaco talassa.com

Around 28 species of the world's 80 or so cetaceans have been sighted in the Azores, a global hot spot

Whale watching off Pico

for whale and dolphin watching. From early April to late June daily sightings of these majestic mammals are almost guaranteed. The sperm whale is present all year (see pp16–17).

4 Surfing
Azores Surf Center: azores surfcenter.com

This is an activity that can be enjoyed throughout the year, although surfing conditions in winter are influenced by swells from the north, persistent depressions and cold fronts. Summer is dominated by waves from the south whipped up by tropical storms. The surf schools on São Miguel are professionally run and highly regarded.

5 Walking and Hiking
Aventour – Azores Adventures: www.aventour.pt

Following the trails that crisscross the nine islands is one of the most rewarding ways to get to know the Azores. Amble inland for magnificent cloud-scudded peaks, verdant valleys and ancient craters that cup tranquil lakes. Lining the coast are precipitous sea cliffs, shallow lagoons and mysterious lava plains (see pp46–7).

6 Bird-watching
SMATUR: www.smatur.pt

The Azores are globally recognized as a bird-watching destination for some species (see pp52–3). Ornithologists and "twitchers" flock to the islands to spot scarce residents such as the Azores bullfinch and Monteiro's storm petrel. The autumn migration is a particularly rewarding period, especially on Flores and Corvo.

7 ## Cycling and Mountain Biking

Geo-Fun: www.geo-fun.com
Riding around the Azores takes visitors through quiet country lanes and rolling pastures. Freewheel the coast and discover natural rock pools and beaches (see pp44–5).

 8 ## Canyoning
WestCanyon: www.west canyon.pt

Wading through streams and abseiling down waterfalls and canyons appeals to many outdoor adventurers. Because of their remote locations, São Miguel, São Jorge and Flores are especially good for this activity.

Canyoning down a steep cliff

 9 ## Horse Riding
Azoresgo: www.azoresgo.com

Saddle up and tour the islands on horseback. Trotting down trails along the coast or through ancient laurisilva forests is a wonderful experience. A number of rural hotels combine a stay with equestrian activities.

 10 ## Sailing
Sail Azores Yacht Charter: www.sailazores.pt

Navigating the archipelago by yacht is exhilarating, almost akin to following in the footsteps of earlier Portuguese explorers (see p36). First-rate marina infrastructure plus numerous sheltered bays and inlets provide safe havens along the way.

TOP 10 SPECIAL INTEREST ACTIVITIES

Batalha golf course, São Miguel

1 Geotourism
www.naturfactor.com
Go underground with speleologists for tours of Pico's caves and grottoes.

2 Climbing and Rappelling
www.bootla.pt
Climb and descend geological wonders under expert supervision.

3 Hot-air Ballooning
www.comunicair.pt
Float over breathtaking volcanic scenery in perfect weather conditions.

4 Paragliding
www.asassaomiguel.com
An annual paragliding festival is held in August at Sete Cidades (see pp14–15).

5 Golf
www.azoresgolfislands.com
There's a choice of three courses: Batalha and Furnas on São Miguel, and Terceira.

6 Big-game Fishing
www.sportfishingazores.com
The fishing season runs from July to mid-October. Fish quotas are regulated.

7 Coasteering
www.azoreanactiveblueberry.com
Explore the water's edge by scrambling over, climbing up or swimming along a rocky, sometimes cut-off coastline.

8 Health and Wellbeing
Termas do Carapacho: (295) 714 212
Soak in mineral-rich waters to ease rheumatism and skin disorders.

9 Stand Up Paddle (SUP)
www.azoressupadventures.com
SUP on the crater lakes or the sea and discover picturesque coves and grottoes.

10 Jet Skiing
www.giganteexpeditions.com
The aquatic "motorbike" provides an adrenaline rush for watersports enthusiasts with a need for speed.

🔟 Birdlife

A flock of roseate terns catching fish from the ocean off Graciosa

1 Azores Bullfinch

Distinguished by its black cap, face, wings and tail, this diminutive bird, known locally as *priolo*, is the most threatened and second-rarest passerine in Europe. It is endemic to the Azores but confined solely to São Miguel, specifically between Serra da Tronqueira and Vale das Furnas in the eastern region *(see p70)*.

2 Monteiro's Storm Petrel

This is the smallest seabird found in the archipelago. Identified by its broad wings, square tail and prominent diagonal wing bar, the species breeds only on two islets off Graciosa: Ilhéu de Baixo and Ilhéu da Praia, considered the largest colony of these birds in the world with approximately 100 pairs *(see p83)*.

3 Azores Grey Wagtail

These lively and inquisitive birds, known for habitually flicking their tails in a characteristic bobbing motion, thrive across all habitats here – they have even been spotted near the summit of Pico. The male of this endemic subspecies can be identified by its black throat; the female's is white.

Azores grey wagtail

4 Roseate Tern

A sleek, handsome seabird with long tail-streamers, this is a summer migrant and is seen throughout the Azores from April to July, when it breeds. Nesting is most abundant on Santa Maria, Graciosa and Flores *(see p99)*, particularly on islets such as Ilhéu de Maria Vaz.

5 Atlantic Canary

Vivid yellow-green plumage with chestnut-brown streaks identifies this small passerine, one of the most colourful in the Azores. Known also as the island canary or wild canary, it is common on all the islands.

6 Common Buzzard

A subspecies endemic to the Azores, this is the archipelago's only resident bird of prey. Smaller than its mainland counterpart, it can be seen in coastal areas and mountainous regions, except the Western Group of islands. Early settlers mistook this bird for a goshawk, which is *açor* in Portuguese, or in plural *açores*. Hence came the collective name for the nine islands *(see p36)*.

7 Azores Quail

Patience and luck are required to spot this shy ground-nesting game bird, which breeds in meadows and fields. The tiny Azores quail is a year-round resident and a native of the archipelago commonly sighted on Terceira (see p83). It is often heard rather than seen, the distinctive quick-fire "wet-my-lips" call emanating from tall grass or cereal fields.

8 Goldcrest
Out of the three endemic subspecies in the Azores it is the Santa Maria goldcrest (see p73) that has captured ornithologists' imagination. The smallest bird in Europe, the goldcrest is restless and hyperactive. The orange crown of the male and the lemon-yellow crest of the female are a bright contrast against the drab, olive-green tones of their upperparts.

9 Cory's Shearwater
One of the strangest sounds likely to be heard during summer nights in the Azores is the constricted, gurgling call of the Cory's shearwater. The birds are seen between March and mid-November, and their raucous cackling marks the breeding season, when they nest in colonies on sea cliffs and rocky outcrops.

A Cory's shearwater taking flight

10 Atlantic Yellow-Legged Gull
The interisland ferries offer excellent vantage points to admire this heavy-set seabird, which has a loud nasal "laugh". Abundant throughout the archipelago, this year-round resident can be easily spotted on landfills and pastureland. Bright yellow legs differentiate it from similar species such as lesser black-backed and herring gulls. Nesting season lasts from mid-March to early May.

TOP 10 ENDEMIC FLOWERING PLANTS

Azorean bellflower

1 Azorean Bellflower (Azorina vidalii)
Rare coastal perennial found across the archipelago except Graciosa and Faial. Flowers May–October.

2 Azorean Holly (Ilex perado azorica)
Subspecies found on all islands except Graciosa. Dispersed in the laurisilva forest, normally above 500 m (1,600 ft).

3 Azorean Blueberry (Vaccinium cylindraceum)
Deciduous shrub with narrow leaves and red flowers. Found on all islands.

4 Azorean Laurustinus (Viburnum treleasei)
Diminutive evergreen shrub noted for its pinkish-white corolla. Blossoms in spring everywhere, except on Graciosa.

5 Azorean Heather (Erica azorica)
Embellished with flowers of green petals and shades of purple. Common on coastal cliffs up to 1,500 m (5,000 ft).

6 Azorean Ivy (Hedera azorica)
Evergreen climbing plant found in dense bush. Flowers are in small umbels.

7 Azorean Dwarf Mistletoe (Arceuthobium azoricum)
Found only on Graciosa, Pico, Faial and Terceira. Characterized by yellow-green stems and paired conical leaves.

8 Azorean Cherry (Prunus azorica)
Rare subspecies with scented flowers that look striking. Found on all islands, except Santa Maria, Graciosa, Flores and Corvo.

9 Oleaceae (Picconia azorica)
Evergreen shrub distinguished by a white corolla and ink-blue oval berries. Does not thrive on Graciosa.

10 Azores Butterfly Orchid (Platanthera micrantha)
Rare plant with pale yellow-green flowers found on all islands, except Graciosa. Seen mostly above 200 m (656 ft).

🔟 Restaurants

① Mesa d'Oito
Signature dishes at this romantic bijou eatery include sirloin steak with *alheira* (pork sausage), sweet potato and crisp vegetables. An extensive wine list takes in the finest regions of Portugal. This is a place to linger over outstanding food *(see p75)*.

② A Traineira
The name of this restaurant alludes to its almost exclusively sea-food menu – *traineira* is Portuguese for trawler, and the daily catch lands on the nearby harbour quayside. Patrons are greeted with the aroma of fresh fish grilled to perfection. The local cheese – *queijo da ilha* – served with corn bread, makes for a delicious starter *(see p103)*.

③ Genuíno
Owner Genuíno Madruga, the acclaimed Portuguese yachtsman who has twice circumnavigated the globe solo, often regales diners with tales of his high sea exploits. The restaurant displays the memorabilia collected during his voyages, and the menu has a suitably nautical flavour. Admire the lovely views of Porto Pim from here *(see p97)*.

④ Anfiteatro
Contemporary cuisine is prepared with pizzazz at this water-front venue. The seasonal menu honours traditional Azorean cuisine but draws on modern techniques and international flavours. The

A pork dish served at Anfiteatro

wine list offers some of the grandest labels in Portugal. Anfiteatro also hosts the prestigious "10 Fest" gourmet food festival *(see p75)*.

⑤ Cais da Angra
The unbeatable location overlooking the marina is accentuated by huge picture windows. Highly regarded for its artisan take on regional Portuguese cuisine, the kitchen also surprises with Asiatic and North African flavours *(see p85)*.

⑥ Pôr do Sol
Built from basalt stone, this evocative farmhouse restaurant set in rolling pastureland is the epitome of rustic. Decorated with antique ceramics, iron pots and pans and the odd farming implement, this is the place to sample home-style cuisine – rich hearty food served up on glazed earthenware plates *(see p103)*.

Charming, rustic exterior of Pôr do Sol

7 Ancoradouro

The "anchorage" is a seafood hot spot offering fine dining in a boathouse-like setting. The menu lists a veritable ocean harvest, cuisine best sampled on the basalt terrace, which offers a panorama of Faial across the channel. Order the *espetada de peixe* (barbecued fish) and muse over the arm-long wine list *(see p97)*.

8 Fornos de Lava

Galician chef Joaquin Alvarez adds authentic Iberian flourishes to the traditional Azorean food served here. The menu features home-style meat and fish dishes, accompanied by fresh, organically grown vegetables. On clear days, the restaurant affords magnificent views of neighbouring Pico and Faial *(see p97)*.

The colourful dining room at Alcides

9 Alcides

This noted family-run restaurant has been dishing up *bife à Alcides* – prime steak garnished with red pepper and garlic – since it opened in 1955. Tables are set against scarlet walls under a vaulted lava-stone ceiling. A huge canvas by the celebrated Domingos Rebelo *(see p37)* enriches the decor *(see p75)*.

10 Quinta das Grotas

Take a taxi to this stone-clad restaurant located in the countryside. The cuisine leans towards hearty rustic food, oven baked or slow roasted to perfection. The atmosphere is particularly homely in winter, especially if it is damp and blustery outside *(see p85)*.

TOP 10 CAFÉS AND BARS

Quirky wall decor at 3/4 Café

1 3/4 Café
This unpretentious, graffiti-walled café-bar serves snacks by day before turning up the music at night *(see p74)*.

2 Arco 8
A bar and gallery exuding bohemian spirit, Arco 8 is also an esteemed visual and performing arts venue *(see p74)*.

3 Sports One Café
MAP U2 ▪ **Rua Diário dos Açores, Ponta Delgada, São Miguel** ▪ **(296) 308 500**
Pool tables and TV screens furnish Hotel Talisman's *(see p116)* English-style pub.

4 Chaminé Club
MAP E2 ▪ **EN1-2A, São Pedro, Santa Maria** ▪ **(917) 212 490**
This fashionable nightclub and music bar starts warming up after midnight.

5 Birou Bar
The centrally located Birou Bar is known for its origami ceiling decor *(see p84)*.

6 Pub Bar Vila Sacramento
Hugely popular, this nightspot is also known as the Good Music Club after its much-admired DJ sets *(see p84)*.

7 Koppus Bar
This vibrant bar attracts a young local crowd. Live music at weekends pulls in a wider audience *(see p96)*.

8 Cella Bar
Set on the coast, the lovely Cella Bar received an international design award for its stylish architecture *(see p97)*.

9 Peter Café Sport
This place is world famous for one drink: the coveted gin and tonic mixed with passion fruit juice *(see p96)*.

10 Lucino's
Open all day for snacks and light meals, Lucino's livens up after dark *(see p103)*.

🔟 Traditional Azorean Cuisine

Flavourful *caldeirada de peixe*

1 Caldeirada de Peixe

The Azores are highly regarded for the variety of fish, and this stew can be made using a range of local fish including grouper, bream and red snapper, as well as prawns and shellfish. Potato, onion, garlic, tomato, white wine and seasoning are also added.

2 Sopa do Espírito Santo

Soup of the Holy Spirit is prepared during the annual Festas do Espírito Santo celebrations (see p62). It is a delicious and hearty broth made using vegetables and meats, seasoned with mint, bay leaves and garlic. Thick slices of buttered cornbread soak up the flavours. Recipes differ from island to island, but the result is always ladled out from a huge tureen.

3 Pudim de Chá Verde dos Açores

Given that the Azores have the only tea estates in Europe, this chilled dessert is unique. It is made with green tea leaves harvested at Gorreana (see p68), and the recipe retains all the nutrients and anti-oxidants, despite the milk and sugar.

4 Sopa de Funcho

Simple and healthy, fennel soup is a flavoursome starter to many an Azorean meal. The whole plant is used, cut to bite-size pieces. Onion, potato, tomato and carrot lend weight. Some cooks add *feijão vermelho* (red beans) to thicken the texture.

5 Pudim de Queijo da Ilha

Soft, smooth and creamy, this heavenly pudding, or flan, is prepared using cheese from São Jorge, along with eggs, natural yogurt and a deliciously nutty caramel sauce. It is an ideal choice after a hearty dinner.

6 Alcatra

Emblematic of Terceira, this traditional pot roast is prepared using *alcatra* (rump) steak marinated in Vinho de Cheiro, a white wine from the Isabella grape. A key ingredient is smoked bacon. Seasoned with allspice and baked in a clay pot, this is one of the most aromatic Azorean dishes.

Alcatra in a clay pot

7 Lapas Grelhadas

Grilled *lapas* (limpets) are a traditional delicacy and can be enjoyed year-round. This dish is usually prepared as an appetizer, and baked with garlic and lemon juice. Another variation is *arroz de lapas* – risotto garnished with parsley. Santa Maria restaurants often serve *lapas de molho Afonso* – braised limpets in a spicy sauce.

Lapas grelhadas, made using limpets

Locals preparing *cozido das Furnas*

8 Cozido das Furnas

Huge pots of *cozido* (stew) are lowered into the hot, volcanic ground next to the beautiful Lagoa das Furnas. After 7 hours of cooking in the earthy ovens, the pots – full of chicken, beef, pork, black pudding, kale, white cabbage, sweet potato, yam and carrot – are ceremoniously raised and sent to nearby restaurants, where the flavoursome assortment is served to diners (see p19).

9 Polvo Guisado

Octopus stewed with wine, onions and red pepper paste, this is one of the archipelago's most representative culinary specialities. Each island has its own variation, with oven roast potatoes also finding room on the plate. Either way, it is a beautifully textured, rich and appetizing seafood dish.

10 Morcela com Ananás

An Azorean staple, the classic preprandial black pudding with pineapple is an inspired combination. The "pudding" is, in fact, grilled blood sausage. It can be sliced broadly and topped with the caramelized fruit, or offered cubed and skewered cocktail-style. Another variation is a flower presentation where a ring of pineapple, sculpted as petals, surrounds a circular slice of sausage.

TOP 10 WINES AND LIQUEURS

1 Arinto dos Açores by António Maçanita
António Maçanita, highly regarded for his mainland Alentejo wines, created this punchy Pico white (see pp32–3).

2 Cancela do Porco
Balanced acidity holds the flavours of this white, made from Verdelho grapes grown on Pico (see pp32–3).

3 Frei Gigante
Named after friar Pedro Gigante, this straw-coloured wine with a fruity flavour is a Pico island classic (see pp32–3).

4 Pedras Brancas
Several wines are available from this Graciosa estate, as well as *aguardente* (clear brandy or "fire water"), distilled in copper tanks (see p82).

5 Da Resistência Branca
Ripe and creamy with hints of honey and plum, this excellent white is pure Verdelho grape (see p78).

6 Chico Maria
Fortified sweet wine produced from Verdelho grapes. Available in dry, medium-dry and sweet styles (see p77).

7 Vinho Generoso
Individually numbered wine bottled in decorative stoneware fired and glazed by artist Renato Costa e Silva (see p77).

8 Aguardente Velhíssima Vínica Mulher de Capote
At a potent 40 per cent, this premier spirit is regarded as the best "fire water" in the Azores (see p71).

9 Maracuja Gourmet
Passion fruit liqueur noted for its pleasant aroma and intense flavour. A favourite island-wide tipple (see p71).

10 Queen of the Islands
A luxuriously smooth and creamy liqueur made with milk from the islands and flavoured with anisette (see p71).

A range of Azorean liqueurs

TOP 10 Places to Shop

1 Cooperativa de Artesanato de Santa Maria

MAP F2 ■ Santo Espírito, Santa Maria ■ (296) 884 888 ■ Closed Sat (from 2pm) & Sun

The artisans of this historic cooperative are renowned throughout the Azores for their weaving skills. On most days nimble-fingered women can be seen creating beautifully patterned bedspreads and blankets. Their hand-woven costumes embody the island's rural character.

Blue-and-white ceramic plate

2 Adega A Buraca

MAP M2 ■ Estrada Regional 35, Santo António, Pico ■ (292) 642 119

Wines, brandies and liqueurs from across the islands, plus jams, breads, cheeses and biscuits are available at this farmhouse delicatessen. Traditionally styled, the rustic ambiance is complemented by the private museum brimming with antique farming tools and vintage machine parts.

3 Parque Atlântico

There are over 80 stores and boutiques, a food court and a multiplex cinema in this impressive shopping mall. The "Atlantic" theme is appropriately conveyed in the shape of an original whaling boat in full sail displayed on the ground floor (see p71).

4 Cerâmica Vieira

The Azores' only manufacturer of glazed pottery, Cerâmica Vieira has been family-owned since its foundation in 1862. Visitors can watch the potters at work before browsing the outstanding tiles and tableware, with many pieces decorated in the traditional blue-and-white brushstroke style known as Louça da Lagoa (see p71).

5 Maria da Assunção Nunes de Azevedo

MAP R6 ■ Estrada Regional, Fazenda das Lajes, Flores ■ (292) 593 256

A much-loved local resident, Maria spends hours making bouquets and rosettes from the dyed pith of hydrangeas. She also uses fish scales to shape equally exquisite blooms (see p60). Passed down from generation to generation, this is a skill she is eager to demonstrate to passers-by, and the delicate miniatures are all for sale.

6 Açorbordados

Needlework of the highest order is produced at this modest studio, founded in 1945. Ornate baby bibs, bread cloths and bottle aprons, all hand embroidered using traditional techniques, are available to purchase (see p82).

7 Loja Peter Café Sport

A preppy-nautical theme runs through the collection of apparel, branded with the café's distinctive logo. Clothing includes T-shirts, jumpers and windcheaters. Also on sale

Whaling boat at Parque Atlântico

are posters taken from the famous photograph of "Neptune" during a storm – a monster wave crashing over a headland, the outline of which resembled the god of the sea *(see p96)*.

⑧ Louvre Michaelense

The sense of nostalgia at this quaint, wood-lined emporium is tangible. Old-fashioned glass-fronted wall cabinets are filled with teas, spices, canned goods and ceramics. Displays of tempting cakes and pastries, radiant in the glow of retro Edison light bulbs, line the counter. Pause for coffee before purchasing one of their quirky handcrafted souvenirs *(see p71)*.

Vintage decor at Louvre Michaelense

⑨ Uniqueijo

Visitors do not have to join a guided tour of this cheese factory to buy rich, aromatic São Jorge cheese, but doing so makes it much more fun. There are several varieties on offer: from those aged for three, four and seven months to the mature two-year-old special, which can be identified by its black label *(p92)*.

⑩ Adega e Cooperativa Agrícola da Ilha Graciosa

Graciosa's wine and agricultural cooperative produces the much admired Pedras Brancas range of wines, notably the white VQPRD. Another favourite tipple is Angelica, but for a real kick try the Vínica, their robust *aguardente*. The estate also cultivates garlic and melon. All produce can be sampled and bought at the farmhouse store *(see p81)*.

TOP 10 PLACES TO BUY REGIONAL BREADS, CAKES AND SWEETS

Traditional *queijadas do Pico*

1 Café Atlântida: São Miguel
Bolos Lêvedos
Sweet, flat soft rolls. The most authentic made in Furnas *(see pp18–19)*.

2 Vila Franco do Campo: São Miguel
Queijadas da Vila Franco do Campo!
Cakes that originated in the 17th century from a recipe handed down by nuns.

3 Cooperativa de Artesanato de Santa Maria: Santa Maria
Biscoitos de Orelha
Rounded textured biscuits resembling the shape of an ear *(orelha)*.

4 O Forno: Terceira
Bolos Dona Amélia
Spicy cakes topped with icing sugar. Named after Portugal's last queen.

5 Casa Museu João Tomáz Bettencourt: Graciosa
Pasteis de Arroz
Cakes made from rice and egg white and flavoured with almond *(see p81)*.

6 Associação de Artesãos: Graciosa
Queijadas da Graciosa
Star-shaped, traditional version of the Portuguese *queijadas* pastry *(see p84)*.

7 Cooperativa de Artesanato Senhora da Encarnação: São Jorge
Espécies
Ribbed cookies baked with *espécies* (spices) such as cinnamon and anise.

8 Dulçores: São Jorge
Rosquilhas de Aguardente
Flower-shaped delicacies in which *aguardente* is added to eggs and flour.

9 Aromas & Sabores: Pico
Bolo Baleeiro
Pico's very own whaler's cake, crammed full of honey with cinnamon flavours.

10 Linu Pastelaria e Padaria: Pico
Queijadas do Pico
A regional variation of sweet *queijadas*, with goat's cheese adding a sour edge.

🔟 Arts and Crafts

1 Fish Scales

A handicraft passed down through generations, the art of turning fish scales into decorative flower clusters requires a high degree of skill. The scales are first dyed and then shaped into delicate petals or leaves with scissors. At the Escola Regional de Artesanato on Pico (see p93) visitors can watch the entire process and admire the colourful, palm-sized bouquets on display.

Decorative flowers made of fish scales

2 Lapinhas

These authentic miniature nativity scenes are set within domes or glass boxes. Created using small figures of painted pottery, fragments of rock, tiny sea shells and moss, flowers and plants, these beautiful and intricate cribs first appeared on the archipelago in the 17th century.

3 Weaving

Using wool, linen or cotton, traditional weaving – which is still done on antique hand-worked looms across the Azores – is represented by the wonderful blankets, handbags and quilts produced at the Cooperativa de Artesanato Nossa Senhora da

Hand-woven traditional handicraft

Encarnação (see p92). The cooperative's ponto alto-style (relief stitch) bedspreads have their origins in the 16th century.

4 Ceramics and Earthenware

Contributing significantly to the Azorean cultural identity, the most emblematic traditional pottery includes simple unglazed pieces such as the bilha (clay jug) and alguidar (bowl). Founded in 1862, Cerâmica Vieira (see p71) is the only manufacturer of ceramic pottery in the Azores. Clay is moulded on the potter's wheel and everything is hand-painted.

5 Violas

Two heart-shaped soundholes distinguish the viola da terra as a unique Azorean musical instrument. The 12-string handmade guitar has a separate fingerboard inlaid in the soundboard, with the bridge ending in bird-like figures. The regional guitars of São Mateus and Santa Cruz on Graciosa are especially decorative.

6 Scrimshaw

Dating from the 19th century and synonymous with Azorean whaling heritage, scrimshaw refers to scrollwork and carvings created by whalers using the bones and teeth of whales. Once widely practised, the tradition has almost disappeared with the diminishing supply of whales' teeth. It is now illegal to take scrimshaw and whalebone products out of Portugal. The Museu de Scrimshaw (see p26) has a collection of rare engraved examples on display.

7 Basalt Jewellery

An example of modern Azorean handicraft, jewellery incorporating basalt rock works both as a fashion accessory and as a symbolic element, like a talisman. Formed from the rapid cooling of basaltic lava, the rock's characteristic sooty hue and pitted texture complements the polished surface of gold or silver (see p71).

8 Corn Husk Dolls

Early settlers used wheat straw, wood and other plant matter as raw material to create various decorative artifacts. These included *bonecas de folhelho* – dolls crafted from cornhusks. Still made today, the beautiful figurines are indicative of the islands' agricultural heritage.

Dolls made from cornhusks

9 Fig Tree Pith Carvings

Incredible dexterity and patience are required to produce fig pith art. Using the soft, fragile pith tissue from the wild fig tree, skilled practitioners produce anything from delicate floral compositions to miniature caravels in full sail. Carvings can be seen on display at the Museu da Horta (see p26).

10 Embroidery

The style of embroidery varies between islands. *Matiz* stitchwork from São Miguel dates back to the early 1930s and has lovely blue floral and campestral motifs. On Terceira, look for pieces created using the exquisite Richelieu stitch. Faial is known for unusual wheat straw embroidery on black tulle.

TOP 10 SOUVENIRS

1 Soft Toy Whales
Louvre Michaelense: Ponta Delgada, São Miguel
Hand-stitched, cute and cuddly cetaceans in varied patterned fabrics.

2 Tea
Plantações de Chá Gorreana: Gorreana, São Miguel
Varieties of black and green teas from the only tea plantation in Europe.

3 Regional Sweets
Cooperativa de Artesanato de Santa Maria: Santo Espírito, Santa Maria
Home-made *biscoitos de orelha* and other goodies from the archipelago.

4 Ceramics
Azulart de Aurélia: Angra do Heroísmo, Terceira
Glazed pottery, such as wall clocks and decorated tiles, made by local artists.

5 Lacework
Associação de Artesãos: Santa Cruz da Graciosa, Graciosa
Hats, scarves and cowls fashioned from intricate crochet, and handmade embroidered lace tablemats.

6 Cheeses
Uniqueijo: Beira, São Jorge
Choice Azores cheeses, including Queijo São Jorge, the connoisseur's favourite.

7 Wines
Adega A Buraca: Santo António, Pico
Verdelho Original, a zesty white from the UNESCO-protected Pico vineyards.

8 Wickerwork
Escola de Artesanato do Capelo: Capelo, Faial
Traditional products for sale, including handmade wicker baskets.

9 Flowers From the Pith of Hydrangeas
Casa Zélia Almeida: Lajes, Flores
Locally made replica flower bouquets.

10 Wooden Door Locks
Casa de José Mendonça de Inês: Estrada do Caldeirão, Corvo
Traditional wooden door locks carved by local craftsman José Mendonça de Inês.

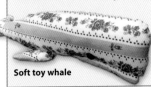

Soft toy whale

 Traditional Festivals

1 Festas do Espírito Santo
All islands ▪ Every Sun for seven weeks after Easter

The archipelago's most important festivals are associated with the Espírito Santo (Holy Spirit). A villager is crowned *imperador* (emperor) and presides over the colourful ceremonies. On the seventh Sunday, soup *(see p56)* and bread are distributed from an *império* (chapel).

Crown, Festas do Espírito Santo

2 Senhor Santo Cristo dos Milagres
MAP U2 ▪ São Miguel ▪ 5th Sun after Easter

Ponta Delgada's celebration honouring the Lord Holy Christ of Miracles is the largest religious festival in the Azores. It is centred on the 16th-century Convento de Nossa Senhora da Esperança *(see p41)*, and features a town procession where the revered figure of Senhor Santo Cristo dos Milagres is carried over streets paved with a fabulous floral tableaux.

3 Festas Sanjoaninas
MAP M6 ▪ Terceira ▪ Nearest Friday to 24 Jun

Mirroring the Portuguese mainland's Festas dos Santos Populares (Festivals of the Popular Saints) tradition, Terceira honours São João (St John) by hosting a huge costumed parade in Angra do Heroísmo *(see pp20–21)*. The dancing and singing draws on age-old customs and folklore.

Senhor Santo Cristo dos Milagres

4 Festa do Emigrante
MAP R6 ▪ Lajes das Flores, Flores ▪ 3rd weekend in Jul

While acknowledging the Holy Spirit with an allegorical procession, this festival is essentially a homecoming party for thousands of Azorean migrants who return to the islands for the summer break. Fringe events include literary talks, art exhibitions and sporting tournaments.

5 Festa da Senhora da Guia
MAP J3 ▪ Horta, Faial ▪ 1st Sun in Aug

A visual treat, the festival of Nossa Senhora da Guia (Protector of the Fishermen) gathers trawler crews from across the island to lead a procession from Porto Pim to the town centre. It marks the beginning of the Semana do Mar (Sea Week), essentially a yachting regatta, but festivities happen on land too.

6 Festival da Ilha Branca
MAP J5 ▪ Santa Cruz da Graciosa, Graciosa ▪ 2nd week in Aug

As with many fêtes and galas in the Azores, the "White Island" festival merges the religious with the secular. Integrated into the parallel Holy Christ ceremonies, Graciosa lets its hair down with modern Portuguese music that attracts a predominantly young crowd.

Festa da Nossa Senhora da Assunção

MAP E2 ▪ Santa Maria ▪ Mid-Aug

Vila do Porto's *(see p68)* municipal gardens host this festival in which Santa Maria pays homage to its patron saint. Entertainment programmes are accompanied by religious ceremonies that take place in and around the Igreja de Nossa Senhora da Assunção.

8 **Semana dos Baleeiros**

MAP N3 ▪ Lajes do Pico, Pico ▪ Last week in Aug

The Week of the Whalers festival is linked to the worship of Nossa Senhora de Lourdes, the patron saint of whalers. This prestigious event features traditional *fado* music and modern guitar rock performances. However, it is the whaling boat regatta that captures the occasion's true spirit.

Whaling boat regatta, Pico

9 **Romaria de Santo Cristo**

MAP Q2 ▪ São Jorge ▪ 1st Sun in Sep

Romarias (religious pilgrimages) are an important tradition of the Catholic communities here. The Holy Christ procession in Fajã dos Vimes ends at the village's tiny chapel, Capela de São Sebastião, for a celebratory feast.

10 **Festa da Senhora do Bom Caminho**

MAP R4 ▪ Vila do Corvo, Corvo ▪ 2nd weekend in Sep

Announcing the arrival of autumn, this ceremony praises Our Lady of the Good Way, a reference to the figure of the Virgin, which is taken on a procession towards the caldera. Highlights include folk dancing, an open-air Mass and lots of food and wine.

TOP 10 SHOWS AND EVENTS

Red Bull cliff diving contest

1 Azores Wave Week
São Miguel ▪ Last week in Mar ▪ azoressurfcenter.com
Surfing workshop that offers surf clinics, master classes and water safety training.

2 Azores Trail Run
Faial ▪ Last week in May ▪ www.azorestrailrun.com
Cross-country courses that include the 70-km (43-mile) Blue Island Challenge.

3 10 Fest
São Miguel ▪ Mid-Jun ▪ taste.visitazores.com
Modern gourmet dishes prepared by ten chefs at Anfiteatro restaurant *(see p75)*.

4 Semana Cultural das Velas
São Jorge ▪ First week in Jul
Festival showcasing local writers, artists and musicians. It also hosts a yacht race.

5 Walk & Talk
São Miguel ▪ Mid-Jul ▪ www.walktalkazores.org
Cutting-edge urban art festival.

6 Red Bull Cliff Diving
São Miguel ▪ Mid-Jul ▪ www.redbullcliffdiving.com
High-octane extreme sports competition.

7 Santa Maria Blues
Santa Maria ▪ Mid-Jul ▪ www.santamariablues.com
Highly regarded blues festival.

8 Taste in Adegas
Pico ▪ Mid-Jul
Wine tastings at *adegas* (wineries).

9 CIMA/RIC International Canyoning Meeting
Flores ▪ 3rd week in Sep ▪ cima.visitazores.com
Rappel the basalt gorges and waterfalls, and then take part in talks and events.

10 Angrajazz
Terceira ▪ Mid-Oct ▪ angrajazz.com
The archipelago's premier jazz festival.

Azores
Area by Area

The beautiful Lagoa do Fogo amid
lush greenery, São Miguel

🔟 São Miguel and Santa Maria Islands

The largest and the most varied of the nine islands in the Azores, São Miguel offers an ideal introduction to this mid-Atlantic archipelago. Ponta Delgada, the island's principal town, is a cosmopolitan base for exploring the volcanic landscape of the interior. Equally alluring is the coastline of dramatic sea cliffs and headlands. Neighbouring Santa Maria has the Azores' warmest climate, where sunshine nourishes vineyards and pastures, and illuminates sandy bays.

A panoramic view of scenic São Miguel island

SÃO MIGUEL AND SANTA MARIA ISLANDS

0 km 5
0 miles 5

Pilar da Bretanha
Bretanha
Mosteiros (8)
Santa Bárbara
Várzea
Lagoa Azul
Santo António
Sete Cidades
Lagoa das Sete Cidades (1)
Ginetes
Lagoa Verde
Fenais da Luz
Candelária (2)
Capelas (6)
Aflitos (9)
Feteiras
Covoada
Fajã de Cima
(10)
(8)
João Paulo II Airport ✈
São Roque
See Ponta Delgada map, below

1 Top 10 Sights
see pp67–9

(3) 400 metres
RUA M. DE CHAVES
Ponta Delgada (3)
RUA DR. ARISTIDES DA MOTA
R. DE SÃO JOÃO
RUA DO PERU
RUE DR. ARISTIDES DA MOTA
(10)
(2)(1)(5)
RUA T. RESENDES
(4)(1)
(2)
AVE. J. B. MOTA AMARAL
Marina de Ponta Delgada
RUA M. DOS SANTOS
(10)
LARGO DA MATRIZ
(2)
Porto da Ponta Delgada
Portas do Mar
(7)
RUA DE LISBOA
(9)
PRAÇA DO MUNICÍPIO
CPO. DE S. FRANCISCO
AVE. INF. DOM HENRIQUE
(7) 800 metres
(4)

0 metres 500
0 yards 500

1 Lagoa das Sete Cidades
MAP A5 ■ São Miguel

According to local lore, a blue-eyed shepherd boy once fell for a green-eyed princess. Love blossomed but it was a forbidden romance. The heartbroken pair parted, shedding tears that formed Lagoa Azul and Lagoa Verde – the twin blue and green lakes sunk into this volcanic crater. From the Vista do Rei lookout, the crater reveals itself, its rim rising to nearly 300 m (1,000 ft) above the water's surface in places.

2 Ribeira Grande
MAP C5 ■ São Miguel

A sweeping beach, Praia de Santa Bárbara, fronts the island's second-largest town. The historic centre boasts gems such as Igreja da Misericórdia (closed to the public), with its Baroque façade, and Ponte dos Oito Arcos, the bridge of eight arches – a 19th-century landmark. The nearby Arquipélago – Centro de Artes Contemporâneas is an example of daring 21st-century design.

The historic city of Ponta Delgada

3 Ponta Delgada
MAP B6 ■ São Miguel

Narrow cobbled lanes, wide leafy squares and parks characterize the Azores' busiest town. Splendid palaces, Baroque mansions and impressive 16th-century churches and convents enhance the historic urban makeup. The 18th-century Portas da Cidade, the original city gates, reflect the town's maritime heritage. An esplanade links the Renaissance Forte de São Brás at the harbour's western end with the modern Portas do Mar to the east.

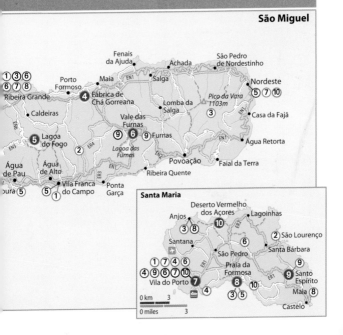

4 Fábrica de Chá Gorreana

MAP D5 ▪ Plantações de Chá Gorreana, São Miguel ▪ (296) 442 349 ▪ Open summer: 8am–8pm Mon–Fri, 9am–8pm Sat & Sun; winter: 8am–7pm Mon–Fri, 9am–7pm Sat & Sun

Founded in 1883, the Gorreana tea estate is the only one of its kind in Europe. Terraces of bushes on hills surround the *fábrica* (factory). The organic shoot tips, hand-picked from April to September, are processed using vintage machinery. Teas can be bought in the showroom.

Tea plantations at Gorreana estate

5 Lagoa do Fogo

MAP D5 ▪ São Miguel

Located within a nature reserve, the expansive "fire lake" is at the bottom of an ancient caldera on Água de Pau Massif. Clinging to its walls is a dense blanket of vegetation. Birdlife flourishes here: Atlantic yellow-legged gulls can be spotted gliding over the crater's lip. The scenic Pico do Barrosa overlook offers the best views.

6 Vale das Furnas

The Furnas Valley meanders over a geothermal landscape of hot springs. On the northern shores of Lagoa das Furnas the volcanic ground is so hot that islanders come here to cook *cozido*, burying the pots in the earth for several hours (see p57). The village of Furnas, surrounded by fumaroles, squats in a huge caldera. The verdant, perfumed 18th-century Parque Terra Nostra is laid out here, textured by trees and plants such as hibiscus and rhododendron. Visitors can bathe in the warm therapeutic waters of the park's swimming pool (see pp18–19).

7 Vila do Porto

MAP E2 ▪ Santa Maria

Unassuming Porto became Vila do Porto after receiving its charter in 1470, the first town in the Azores elevated to such a status. There is little left of Santa Maria's 15th-century capital, save for some weathered façades that would once have turned heads. Still spruce is the 16th-century Forte de São Brás. The engaging Centro de Interpretação Ambiental Dalberto Pombo houses the personal collection of local naturalist Dalberto Pombo, a pioneer in the study of the island's natural heritage (see p72).

8 Praia da Formosa

MAP E2 ▪ Santa Maria

One of the most attractive and popular beaches of the archipelago, Praia da Formosa is hemmed in by steep cliffs, with fields and meadows forming

The inky-blue Lagoa do Fogo

GONÇALO VELHO CABRAL

Credited with the discovery in 1431 of the Ilhéus das Formigas, scattered islets in the Eastern Group of islands, Portuguese explorer Gonçalo Velho Cabral (c.1400–1460) later rediscovered Santa Maria and São Miguel islands. He was appointed Capitão Donatário (lord proprietor) of both islands, the first to hold the newly created title.

a pleasing pastoral backdrop. The half-moon beach of white sand sits in one of the loveliest corners of the island. As an exposed beach and reef break, this is an internationally renowned surf spot; an area is marked off for surfboards. Amenities include changing facilities and showers, and a handy bar-café.

⑨ Santo Espírito
MAP F2 ■ Santa Maria

There are two good reasons to explore this limewashed village: first, the pretty Igreja de Nossa Senhora da Purificação *(see p40)*, and secondly, the Cooperativa de Artesanato de Santa Maria *(see p58)*, a handicrafts cooperative with its own bakery. The home-made bread and *biscoitos de orelha* are irresistible, and the home-spun blankets make ideal souvenirs.

⑩ Deserto Vermelho dos Açores
MAP E2 ■ Santa Maria

One of the most surprising natural phenomena of the archipelago is the "Red Desert of the Azores". This wave-like landscape near Santa Maria's northern shores is referred to as Barreiro da Faneca in Portuguese. It is an arid blanket of Pliocene sediments composed of clay minerals spread over ancient lava flow from Pico Alto, the island's highest point. Smothered by pyroclasts (volcanic fragments), the clay oxidized to produce an environment akin to that of Mars *(see p43)*.

EXPLORING SANTA MARIA ISLAND

[Map showing Santa Maria Island with labels: Anjos, São Pedro, Lagoinhas, Santa Bárbara, Baía de São Lourenço, Pedras de São Pedro, Vila do Porto, Almagreira, Praia, Santo Espírito]

▶ MORNING

Start the day with coffee and *torrada* (toast) at **Garrouchada** *(see p74)* in Vila do Porto. Drive north to ER-1-2 and then turn east to Almagreira. From here it is a short drive south to **Praia** where a glorious beach frames the shallow bay. Dip your toes in the crystalline water before returning to Almagreira. Continue east to **Santo Espírito**. Spend time here admiring the **Igreja de Nossa Senhora da Purificação** *(see p40)* and then browse the handicrafts at the **Cooperativa de Artesanato de Santa Maria** *(see p58)*. Don't forget to try their home-made biscuits *(see p59)*. If you have some time, nip into the nearby **Museu de Santa Maria** *(see p72)*. The scenic ER-3-2 eventually brings you to **Baía de São Lourenço** *(see p72)*. Stop for lunch at one of the **cafés** lining the beachfront.

AFTERNOON

Suitably refreshed, change gear and take ER-2-2 towards Santa Bárbara. This is one of the prettiest drives on the island. After skirting the coast near Lagoinhos the road snakes inland towards São Pedro. Carry on for 10 minutes and then take a right towards Anjos. This village is known for the historic **Capela de Nossa Senhora dos Anjos** *(see p41)* and its association with **Christopher Columbus** *(see p36)*. Later, double back through Pedras de São Pedro. Relive the day over drinks at the **Central Pub** *(see p74)* in Vila do Porto.

See map on pp66–7 ←

The Best of the Rest: São Miguel

1 Vila Franca do Campo
MAP D6 ■ Ilhéu da Vila Franca
ferries Jun–Sep ■ Adm

A timeless air pervades this appealing coastal village. Out to sea is Ilhéu da Vila Franca, the remains of an old volcano. This islet hosts the Red Bull cliff diving competition *(see p63)*.

2 Lagoa do Congro
MAP D6

This lagoon is spellbinding for its ethereal beauty. Reached via a forest trail, the lake's surface resembles a pea-green oval mirror.

3 Serra da Tronqueira
MAP F5 ■ Centro Ambiental do Priolo: Parque da Cancela do Cinzeiro, nr Nordeste ■ centropriolo.spea.pt

The wooded Tronqueira hill range is home to the rare Azores bullfinch *(see p52)*. A visitor centre explains more.

4 Museu Militar dos Açores
MAP U2 ■ Forte de São Brás, Avenida Infante Dom Henrique, Ponta Delgada ■ (296) 304 920 ■ Adm

Examine historical armaments such as the rare palm-sized German Mauser pistol. The 16th-century fort can also be explored.

Cannon, Museu Militar dos Açores

5 Caloura
MAP C6

This seaside retreat is highly regarded for its seafood restaurants *(see p75)*. The natural harbour-side swimming pools provide endless fun, while the 16th-century private chapel and convent can be admired from afar.

6 Oficina-Museu M J Melo
MAP B5 ■ Rua do Loural 56, Capelas ■ (296) 298 202 ■ Closed Sun ■ Adm

Local resident Manuel João Melo built this museum as a 1940s-era street lined with shops and a bar, recreated using period furniture and fittings.

Miradouro Ponte do Arnel, Nordeste

7 Nordeste
MAP F5

Explore the eastern tip of the island and Serra da Tronqueira from this scenic town. The lookout, Miradouro Ponte do Arnel, peers over a craggy headland topped by a lighthouse.

8 Arquipélago Centro de Artes Contemporâneas
MAP C5 ■ Rua Adolfo Coutinho de Medeiros, Ribeira Grande ■ Adm ■ arquipelagocentrodeartes. azores.gov.pt

This former tobacco factory has been transformed into the archipelago's premier visual and performing arts venue, with an exhibition space, a high-tech stage and a multimedia centre.

9 Torre Sineira
MAP U2 ■ Câmara Municipal, Praça do Município, Ponta Delgada ■ Closed Sat & Sun

The bell tower houses a massive 16th-century bronze bell, the oldest in Azores. Rooftop offers fine views.

10 Sinagoga de Ponta Delgada
MAP U2 ■ Rua do Brum 14–16, Ponta Delgada ■ Closed Sat & Sun

The 19th-century Sahar Hassamain (Gates of Heaven) Synagogue is the oldest in Portugal. It retains its ark, benches, bimah and wall panelling.

Shops: São Miguel

① Louvre Michaelense
MAP U2 ▪ Rua António José D'Almeida 8, Ponta Delgada ▪ (938) 346 886

The feel of a bygone era is immediate at this general store and café. Look for hand-stitched soft toy whales and order green tea and cake *(see p59)*.

② Quintal dos Açores
MAP A5 ▪ Rua da Canadinha 20a, Candelária ▪ quintaldosacores.com

This family business produces jellies, jams, honey, pickles and sauces hand-made on site to traditional recipes.

③ Parque Atlântico
MAP U1 ▪ Rua da Juventude, Ponta Delgada ▪ www.parque atlanticoshopping.pt

A supermarket anchors retail outlets, restaurants, cafés and a multiplex cinema to this shopping mall *(see p58)*.

④ Paulo do Vale
MAP U2 ▪ Rua Machado dos Santos 89, Ponta Delgada ▪ www.paulodovale.com

Skilled goldsmith Paulo do Vale fashions exquisite jewellery from gold, silver and Azorean black lava stone.

⑤ Mercado da Graça
MAP V2 ▪ Rua do Mercado, Ponta Delgada

A rich bounty of exotic produce, such as *annonas* (custard apples) and *inhame das furnas* (yam from Furnas) graces the island's biggest market.

Local produce at Mercado da Graça

⑥ Fábrica de Licores Mulher de Capote
MAP C5 ▪ Rua do Berquó 12, Ribeira Grande ▪ www.mulherdecapote.pt

The liqueurs for sale at this distillery can be sampled as part of a free guided tour of the facility *(see p57)*.

⑦ Liberty Store
MAP C5 ▪ Avenida Dr José Nunes da Ponte, Ribeira Grande ▪ www.island-import.com

Branded imported goods ranging from Maine blueberry muffins to Carolina's American Candies are on offer here.

Pottery on display at Cerâmica Vieira

⑧ Cerâmica Vieira
MAP A6 ▪ Rua das Alminhas, Lagoa ▪ (296) 912 116

Admire the potters at their wheels at this ceramics factory before browsing the showroom. A museum chronicles the business since 1862 *(see p58)*.

⑨ Com Certeza Gourmet
MAP V2 ▪ Rua Dr Francisco Machado Fario e Maia 22, Ponta Delgada ▪ comcerteza.pt

The range of Portuguese wines at this deli is impressive. Condiments include *flor de sal* (sea salt).

⑩ Posto de Turismo-Nordeste
MAP F5 ▪ Rua António Alves de Oliveira, Nordeste ▪ (296) 488 320

This tourist office also sells handicrafts such as cornhusk dolls and hand-embroidered tablecloths *(see p61)*.

See map on pp66–7 ←

Sights: Santa Maria

1 Forte de São Brás
MAP E2 ▪ Largo Sousa e Silva, Vila do Porto

Perched on a bluff overlooking the harbour, this well-preserved 16th-century stronghold houses the chapel of Nossa Senhora da Conceição. Admire the fine sea views from here.

A village along Baía de São Lourenço

2 Baía de São Lourenço
MAP F2 ▪ São Lourenço

The terraced vineyards on the steep cliffs rearing up from São Lourenço Bay add texture to the dramatic perspective. The unique landscape is a protected nature reserve.

3 Capela de Nossa Senhora dos Anjos
MAP D1 ▪ Anjos

Crew members from the *Niña*, a caravel commanded by Christopher Columbus, are believed to have prayed here in 1493 during the voyage home from the New World *(see p41)*.

4 Pedreira do Campo
MAP E2 ▪ Pico Facho

A 100-m (328-ft) wall of pillow lava looms over a rich vein of exposed sediments and oceanic fossils, estimated to be five million years old.

5 Praia
MAP E2

Popular with watersports enthusiasts who are drawn to its shallow bay and the sandy Praia da Formosa *(see pp68–9)*, the village was once guarded from pirates by the long ruined 17th-century Forte de São João Baptista.

6 Pico Alto
MAP E2

At 590 m (1,935 ft), the summit of Santa Maria's highest peak is a tempting proposition for hikers. There is also a poignant reminder of a 1989 plane crash, marked by a memorial.

7 Centro de Interpretação Ambiental Dalberto Pombo
MAP E2 ▪ Rua Teófilo Braga 10–14, Vila do Porto ▪ (296) 206 798 ▪ Open Jun–Sep: 10am–6pm daily; Oct–May: 10am–5pm Tue–Fri, 2–5pm Sat ▪ Adm

A new exhibition hall, the Casa dos Fósseis, adds an exciting dimension to this already excellent environmental interpretation centre.

8 Maia
MAP F2

The near-vertical stone terracing for grapevines on cliffs near Maia's Farol de Gonçalo Velho, a 1920s lighthouse, almost defies gravity. The wine, *vinho da cheiro*, is a popular local tipple.

9 Museu de Santa Maria
MAP F2 ▪ Rua do Museu, Santo Espírito ▪ (296) 884 844 ▪ Open Apr–Sep: 10am–5:30pm Tue–Sun; Oct–Mar: 9:30am–5pm Tue–Sun ▪ Adm

This delightful ethnographic museum displays local curios and antique hand-me-downs. The kitchen earthenware and period costumes stand out.

10 Ribeira de Maloás
MAP E2 ▪ Barreiro da Malbusca

After prolonged rainfall, the bubbling stream trickling over the lip of this enormous basalt column formation becomes a picturesque waterfall.

Outdoor Activities

1 Bird-watching
Gerby Birding:
www.gerbybirding.com
The rare Azores bullfinch is the one to watch on São Miguel. Spotting the equally elusive Santa Maria goldcrest is worth taking the trip to the other island (see pp52–3).

Azores bullfinch

2 Whale Watching
MAP V2 ■ Futurismo:
www.futurismo.pt
Encounters with these majestic mammals are mesmerizing. Several species can be seen throughout the year. Lively dolphins always make the occasions high-spirited and playful (see pp16–17).

3 Surfing
MAP C5 ■ Azores Surf Center:
azoressurfcenter.com
Two beaches on São Miguel stand out: Areais de Santa Bárbara, on the north coast, and Milícias near Ponta Delgada. Santa Maria is home to the Anjos and Formosa beaches.

4 Walking
Azores Trails of Nature:
www.azorestrailsofnature.com
Walking tours are a treat for the senses. Tread a path across an astonishing variety of landscapes – lush pastureland, cratered hills, barren sands and coastal plains.

5 Cycling
SMATUR: www.smatur.pt
Pedal off-road for all-mountain rides and a pure adrenaline rush. The quiet rural lanes of the islands are also ideal for exploring on bikes.

6 Canyoning
MAP E2 ■ Bootlá – Natureza & Aventura: www.bootla.pt
Rappel narrow canyons under waterfalls into hidden lakes. Be prepared to climb, scramble, swim and jump to reach your destination.

7 Diving
MAP E2 ■ Mantamaria Dive Center: divecenter.mantamaria.com
São Miguel and Santa Maria benefit from their proximity to the Dollabarat seamount and Ilhéus das Formigas, two marine reserves teeming with dusky grouper, box ray and amberjack, among other fish (see pp24–5).

8 Horse Riding
MAP C6 ■ Quinta da Terça:
www.quintadaterca.com
Following scenic bridleways astride a purebred Lusitano is an enchanting way to see the Azorean landscape. Exploring on horseback takes riders off the beaten track and the immediacy with nature is quite captivating.

9 Golf
MAP E5 ■ Azores Golf Islands:
www.azoresgolfislands.com
Tee off in the mid-Atlantic at the Batalha golf course, which affords sweeping ocean views. A luxurious volcanic landscape wraps itself around the Furnas course.

The verdant Batalha golf course

10 Sailing
MAP E2 ■ Goldensail: www.goldensailazores.com
Seasoned yachties who have the necessary certification can charter a boat and navigate between the two islands. Landlubbers can choose a themed tour captained by a skipper.

See map on pp66–7 ←

Cafés and Bars

1 3/4 Café
MAP U1 ■ Rua Dr
Guilherme Poças Falcão
10, Ponta Delgada, São
Miguel ■ (962) 815 266
■ Closed Sun & Mon

Soups, hamburgers and
home-made cakes form the
menu here. Nightfall brings
a free-spirited crowd who
appreciate the bar's
alternative vibe (see p55).

Graffiti at the entrance to Arco 8

2 Mascote
MAP V2 ■ Largo da Matriz 62,
Ponta Delgada, São Miguel ■ (296)
284 399

The arched roof of this café, one of
the oldest in Ponta Delgada, was
once part of the original colonnade
that fronted the quayside.

3 Paquete
MAP E2 ■ Praia Formosa, Santa
Maria ■ (296) 884 142

Opposite the Beach Parque leisure
facility (Jun–Sep), this seafront eatery
is popular with beachgoers and hikers.

4 Central Pub
MAP E2 ■ Rua Doutor Luís
Bettencourt 20, Vila do Porto, Santa
Maria ■ (296) 882 513

This jolly, authentic American-style
pub is all about reflecting on the day
with buddies over ice-cold beer.

5 O Forno
MAP F5 ■ Rua de Trás da
Igreja 1a, Nordeste, São Miguel
■ (296) 488 200

Breakfasts, snacks and light meals are
available at this homely establishment.
The hot bread rolls are plated up
straight from the *forno* (oven).

6 TukáTulá Bar
MAP C5 ■ Areal de Santa
Bárbara, Ribeira Grande, São Miguel
■ (296) 477 647

A favourite hang-out for surfers, this
beachfront bar-restaurant is popular
for its savvy design and stunning views.

7 Arco 8
MAP B6 ■ Rua Engenheiro
Abel Ferin Coutinho, Ponta Delgada,
São Miguel ■ (918) 393 580 ■ Closed
Sun & Mon

Providing a platform for high impact
visual arts and live music performances, gallery-cum-bar Arco 8 is
a funky hangout for young creatives –
writers, poets and musicians (see p55).

8 Bar dos Anjos
MAP D1 ■ Lugar dos Anjos,
Anjos, Santa Maria ■ (296) 886 734
■ DA

The "angel's bar" is situated over a
terraced pool complex built around
natural rock pools. Crowded and
animated during the day, evening
brings sundowners and a lighter vibe.

9 Garrouchada
MAP E2 ■ Rua Doutor Luís
Bettencourt 25, Vila do Porto, Santa
Maria ■ (296) 883 038 ■ DA

Unwind on the pleasant terrace over
morning coffee and cake, or drop by
later for a delectable seafood platter.
Dinner here is a hearty affair. Book
ahead during the summer season.

10 Lava Jazz Bar
MAP B6 ■ Rua António de
Medeiros 6, Ponta Delgada, São
Miguel ■ (296) 684 097

The toe-tapping jazz at this elegant
venue ups Ponta Delgada's nightlife
tempo. National line-ups and invited
musicians from overseas deliver sets
layered with multitextured rhythms.

Restaurants

1 Alabote

MAP C5 ■ Rua East Providence 68, Ribeira Grande, São Miguel ■ (296) 473 516 ■ Closed Wed ■ €€

Alabote has garnered praise for its creative take on traditional cuisine.

2 Alcides

MAP U2 ■ Rua Hintze Ribeiro 67, Ponta Delgada, São Miguel ■ (296) 629 884 ■ Closed Sun ■ DA ■ €€

Celebrated for its steaks, the kitchen is also noted for its seafood *(see p55)*.

3 Caloura Bar-Esplanade

MAP C6 ■ Porta da Caloura, São Miguel ■ (296) 913 283 ■ €€

Crashing waves, cackling gulls and the tang of grilled fish set the scene here.

4 Mesa d'Oito

MAP E2 ■ Rua Teófilo de Braga 31, Vila do Porto, Santa Maria ■ (296) 882 107 ■ €€

The dining room of the Charming Blue Hotel boasts a superb menu *(see p54)*.

5 Atlântico

MAP D6 ■ Rua Vasco da Silveira 10, Vila Franca do Campo, São Miguel ■ (296) 583 360 ■ Closed Mon, Dec & Jan ■ €€

Tables on the terrace offer romantic views of Ilhéu da Vila Franca *(see p70)*.

6 O Pipas Churrasqueira

MAP E2 ■ Rua da Olivença 11, Vila do Porto, Santa Maria ■ (296) 882 000 ■ Closed Sun ■ €

The chicken served at this grill house is top-notch; dab it with *piri-piri*.

> **PRICE CATEGORIES**
>
> For a three-course meal for one with half a bottle of wine (or equivalent meal), taxes and extra charges.
>
> **€** under €20   **€€** €20–40   **€€€** over €40

Modest interior of Gazcilda

7 Anfiteatro

MAP V2 ■ Portas do Mar, Ponta Delgada, São Miguel ■ (296) 206 150 ■ DA ■ €€€

Reinvented island cuisine and local wine pairing match the stylish, minimalist decor *(see p54)*.

8 Gazcilda

MAP A4 ■ Rua da Ponte 16, Mosteiros, São Miguel ■ (296) 913 283 ■ Oct–mid-Jun: lunch only ■ €

Come here for *polvo assado* – roasted octopus drizzled with red wine sauce.

9 Tony's

MAP E5 ■ Largo da Igreja 5, Furnas, São Miguel ■ (296) 584 290 ■ €

Tony's dishes up the stew cooked underground near Furnas Lake – *cozido das Furnas (see p57)*. It is popular, so book ahead.

10 Rotas

MAP U2 ■ Rua Pedro Homem 49, Ponta Delgada, São Miguel ■ (296) 628 560 ■ €

Scuffed tabletops and odd chairs give this vegetarian restaurant an appealingly disorganised vibe. Expect tofu, quinoa and other healthy items.

Menu made of cloth at Rotas

See map on pp66–7 ←

TOP 10 Terceira and Graciosa Islands

Deriving its name from the fact that it was the third island to be discovered, Terceira is home to the most beautiful town in the Azores: Angra do Heroísmo. The historic island's interior impresses with an ancient volcanic landscape of plunging caves, mysterious cones and sweeping massifs. Wines are cultivated from black, serrated lava plains and the island-wide *impérios* – the dainty chapels of the Holy Spirit – are some of the most ornate in the archipelago. Peppered with scarlet-topped windmills, the rural idyll that is Graciosa, the Azores' second smallest island, has a pleasant yesteryear appeal. Terraced vineyards cling perilously to forbidding sea cliffs, the realm of gregarious seabirds. Below this precious environment, a volcanic cavern shelters a freshwater lake. The entire island is a UNESCO designated Biosphere Reserve.

Obelisk at Angra do Heroísmo

TERCEIRA AND GRACIOSA ISLANDS

1 Angra do Heroísmo

Exploring this Terceira town – a UNESCO World Heritage Site – is an enchanting experience. There is a remarkable portfolio of historic property, including churches, convents and balconied palaces, all in pristine condition. Visit Angra do Heroísmo to see not one but many towns, shaped over centuries by European, American and Asian cultural influences *(see pp20–21)*.

2 Serra de Santa Bárbara

MAP L5 ■ **Centro de Interpretação da Serra de Santa Bárbara, Estrada das Doze, Terceira** ■ (295) 403 800 ■ Open Jun–Sep: 10am–6pm daily; Oct–May: 10am–5pm Tue–Fri, 2–5:30pm Sat ■ Adm

The Santa Bárbara hill range presents visitors with a landscape brushed by heather and juniper. On the summit is a protected nature reserve that hugs a crater – at 1,022 m (3, 353 ft)

this is the island's highest point. The views beyond embrace other islands in the Central Group, anchored in a blue Atlantic. The interpretation centre provides background information.

3 Algar do Carvão

Daylight diminishes as visitors descend this volcanic chimney on Terceira, an astonishing natural phenomenon. The result of an eruption about 2,000 years ago, the vent plunges 100 m (328 ft) below the surface to widen into a series of huge caverns. The conduit drops further and ends in a lake fed by rainwater. A Regional Natural Monument, the lava tube is near the Caldeira de Guilherme Moniz *(see pp30–31)*.

Museu do Vinho dos Biscoitos

4 Museu do Vinho dos Biscoitos

MAP M4 ■ **Canada do Caldeiro, nr Biscoitos, Terceira** ■ (965) 667 324 ■ Open May–Sep: 10–11am & 1–5:30pm Tue–Sun; Oct–Apr: 1:30–4pm Tue–Sat

The Biscoitos winery is renowned for its Verdelho wines – labels such as Da Resistência – and the fortified liqueurs Vinho Generoso and Chico Maria. Custodian of the on-site museum Luís Brum imparts the history behind the antique artifacts used in the cultivation and picking of grapes. The vineyard tour includes wine tasting.

5 Furna do Enxofre

MAP K6 ■ Centro de Visitantes da Furna do Enxofre, Caldeira da Graciosa, Graciosa ■ (295) 714 009 ■ Open Jun–Sep: 10am–6pm daily; Oct–May: 10am–5pm Tue–Fri, 2–5:30pm Sat ■ Adm

Of great speleological importance, this volcanic cave is one of the most significant geosites in the Azores. Set under the island's caldera, it is 180 m (590 ft) wide and reaches 80 m (262 ft) high in places. The cavern features a convex ceiling with stalactites and mineral deposits, and the floor cups a fumarole. A subterranean lake occupies the deepest part of the cave, the floor of which lies below sea level. There is an interpretative centre and guided tours are offered (see p42).

7 Santa Cruz da Graciosa

MAP J5 ■ Graciosa

Dotted with church spires and, on its outskirts, red-topped basalt windmills Graciosa's main town exudes a bygone charm. Incongruous against this traditional setting is the modern wing of the Museu da Graciosa (see p39). The island's viticulture tradition is upheld at the Pedras Brancas winery. A grand perspective of the area can be had from Monte da Ajuda (see p81).

8 Biscoitos

MAP M4 ■ Terceira

A coastal area synonymous with Verdelho wines, this region is named for the nuggets of solidified black lava deposited after an eruption in 1761 – the oval shapes reminded early settlers of their boat bread, or *biscoito* (biscuit), supply. Wine has been produced here since the 16th century, cultivated from vineyards pocketed within walled enclosures called *curraletas*. It is an intriguing landscape made even more attractive by the enticing natural rock pools (see p44) near the harbour.

Furna do Enxofre volcanic cave

6 Praia da Vitória

MAP P5 ■ Terceira

A wedge of pale sand and a busy marina lend this port a holiday-resort atmosphere. Terceira's second-largest town was once known as Praia, but after the Liberal forces overran the Absolutists here in 1829 (see pp36–7), it was renamed Praia da Vitória to commemorate the victory. The pedestrianized streets leading off the main square, Praça Francisco Ornelas da Câmara, make for rewarding shopping, and some of the archipelago's more elaborate *impérios* are found nearby.

Fishermen's Monument, Praia da Vitória

9 Ilhéu da Praia

MAP K5 ■ Graciosa

Poking out of the water 1 km (half a mile) off the coast of Praia, this tiny basalt islet is home to a variety of seabirds, the Azores' most diverse colony.

Santa Cruz da Graciosa viewed from Monte de Ajuda

A Special Protected Area indicative of Graciosa's UNESCO Biosphere Reserve classification, the ocean-lapped rock attracts many migratory species but the one bird every ornithologist trains their binoculars on is the Monteiro's storm petrel (see p52).

⑩ Termas do Carapacho

MAP K6 ■ Rua Doutor Manuel de Sousa Menezes, Carapacho, Graciosa ■ (295) 714 212 ■ Open Jul–Sep: 10am–7pm Tue–Sun; Oct–Jun: noon–5:30pm Tue & Thu, noon–7pm Wed & Fri, 10am–5pm Sat & Sun ■ Adm

Musculoskeletal and dermatological disorders are treated at this wellness retreat. It uses the island's curative geothermal waters in treatments, and offers a menu that includes float therapy and Vichy showers. After an indulgent soak, pamper yourself with a sleep-inducing massage. There has been a spa on this site since 1750 and the foundations of the original building can still be seen.

THE 1980 EARTHQUAKE

On 1 January 1980 an earthquake measuring 7.2 on the Richter scale struck the Azores. The tremor shook the Central Group of islands, and Terceira bore the brunt. Angra's historic quarter suffered damage but it was Doze Ribeiras (see p80), the village nearest the epicentre, that was worst affected. In all, 61 people perished while 15,000 were made homeless.

A WALK AROUND ANGRA DO HEROÍSMO

▶ **MORNING**

Start your exploration of this fascinating UNESCO World Heritage Site with breakfast at **Verde Maçã Café** (see p84) on Rua Direita. Afterwards, walk to **Palácio dos Capitães Generais** (see p20), the former residence of the island's governor, and join a guided tour of the palace. Next, wander through the **Jardim Duque da Terceira** (see p21), one of the most attractive public gardens in the Azores, and climb the steps to **Outeiro da Memória**, or Memorial Hill (see p21). On a sunny day the panorama over the town is quite uplifting. Retrace your route to the **Convento de São Francisco**, which houses Angra's excellent museum (see p38). Spend an hour here admiring the different collections that illustrate the island's history. With lunchtime approaching, amble back towards Rua Direita for a bite at **A Minha Casa** (see p84).

AFTERNOON

Start the afternoon by visiting the impressive 18th-century **Igreja da Misericórdia** (see p40), its pale blue façade a familiar harbourfront landmark. Stroll along the quayside before heading back into the historic centre. Pick up Rua da Rosa to make your way to the ornate 16th-century **Convento de São Gonçalo** (see p41). From here it is a short jaunt west to **Castelo de São João Baptista** (see p21). Tread the weathered battlements and if you are fortunate, a late-afternoon sun will burnish the views with gold.

See map on pp76–7 ←

The Best of the Rest: Terceira

1 Circuito das Furnas de Enxofre
MAP M5

An interesting diversion, the trail snakes over fumaroles and hot springs. The information panels explain more about the landscape (see p31).

2 Mistérios Negros
MAP M5

The "dark mysteries" are trachyte rock domes bereft of vegetation. Admire these volcanic phenomena on the walk from the Gruta do Natal visitor centre near Lagoa do Negro.

3 Cinco Ribeiras
MAP L5

This pretty village is known for its delicious *vaquinha* cheese (see p82), scenic harbour and the swimming facilities at Ponta das Cinco Ribeiras.

4 Doze Ribeiras
MAP L5

Every year the houses in this village are repainted to herald the Holy Ghost festivities (see p62). This act also marks the 1980 earthquake (see p79).

5 Império da Caridade
MAP P5 ■ Rua do Cruzeiro, Praia da Vitória ■ Closed to the public

The *impérios* (empires) of the Holy Spirit (see p62) are chapel-like structures seen across the Azores. They are especially ornate on Terceira, which has about 70 *impérios*.

6 Serra do Cume
MAP N5 ■ Miradouro da Serra do Cume

At 545 m (1,788 ft), Serra do Cume's highest point offers a splendid view of Praia da Vitória, but it is the stone-walled fields that eyes are drawn to.

7 Ponta das Contendas
MAP P6

The islets around the Contendas promontory harbour seabirds. Nearby, São Sebastião commemorates the 1581 Battle of Salga with a monument.

8 Os Montanheiros
MAP U4

Everything visitors need to know about the Azores' volcanic caves can be found at the Society of Exploration and Speleology headquarters (see p30).

9 Serreta
MAP L5

Explore the village and lighthouse as part of a stroll to Ponta do Raminho. In summer the cliffs come alive with nesting Cory's shearwaters (see p53).

10 Gruta do Natal
MAP M5 ■ Pico Gordo, Reserva Florestal Natural da Serra de Santa Bárbara ■ Open mid-Mar–Oct: pm only ■ Adm

Around 700 m (2,296 ft) in length, this circular lava tube is well signed with explanations that identify the lava formations.

The bright, colourful façade of the Império da Caridade

Attractions: Graciosa

1 Adega e Cooperativa Agrícola da Ilha Graciosa

MAP J5 ▪ Charco da Cruz 12, Santa Cruz da Graciosa ▪ (295) 712 169 ▪ Open 9am–5pm Mon–Fri

Tour the winery before uncorking the wines, which include the flagship VQPRD Pedras Brancas, a bold white with fresh fruit notes *(see p59)*.

2 Moinhos de Vento

MAP K5

Early Flemish settlers left these cylindrical basalt stone windmills with red cupolas. Many have wooden latticed spokes, sometimes with sails.

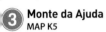

Flemish windmill with red cupola, Graciosa

3 Monte da Ajuda

MAP K5

From this lofty vantage point Santa Cruz da Graciosa resembles a picture postcard. Three chapels, including the Ermida da Nossa Senhora da Ajuda *(see p41)*, occupy the summit.

4 Museu da Graciosa

MAP K5 ▪ Largo Conde de Simas 17, Santa Cruz da Graciosa ▪ (295) 712 429 ▪ Adm

This museum houses local artifacts and curios. Exhibits include a miller's horse-driven grinding stone *(see p39)*.

5 Praia (São Mateus)

MAP K5

Fishing is the main economic activity of this attractive port. The *praia* (beach) nets summertime crowds.

6 Casa Museu João Tomáz Bettencourt

MAP J5 ▪ Rua Eng. Marcelo Bettencourt 8, Guadalupe ▪ (916) 652 2483 ▪ Open 9am–noon & 1–4pm Mon–Fri

The former 19th-century home and general store of a local trader is now a lovely museum. Sweets and local wines can be purchased.

7 Burro Anão da Ilha Graciosa

MAP J5 ▪ Quinta da Esperança Velha, Rua da Esperança Velha 14, Ribeirinha ▪ (911) 001 936

The endangered Graciosa *burro anão* (dwarf donkey) is unique to the island. Franco Ceraolo runs a farm where visitors can get to know these animals.

8 Associação de Artesãos da Ilha Graciosa

MAP J5 ▪ Rua Infante Dom Henrique 50, Santa Cruz da Graciosa ▪ (295) 712 837 ▪ Open 8:30am–4:30pm Mon–Wed

This artisans' association focuses on traditional embroidery. The enthu-siasm of the women matches the quality of their products *(see p82)*.

Ilhéu da Baleia rock formation

9 Ponta da Barca and Ilhéu da Baleia

MAP J4–5

At 23 m (75 ft), the Ponta da Barca lighthouse is the tallest in the Azores. Its tower looms over the headland and the "Whale Islet" rock formation.

10 Reservatório de Água – Atalho

MAP J5 ▪ Rua Engenheiro Manuel Rodrigues de Miranda, Santa Cruz da Graciosa ▪ Open 1:30–5pm Mon–Fri

This 1866-built underground vaulted cistern supplied water to Santa Cruz. Visitors descend via a steep stairwell.

See map on pp76–7

Shops

1 **QB Food Court**
MAP M6 ▪ Caminho do Meio de São Carlos 50, Angra do Heroísmo, Terceira ▪ (295) 333 999
Buy artisan milk and dark chocolates as treats, or create your own gift box at this boutique café-restaurant.

Display window at O Forno

2 **O Forno**
MAP U4 ▪ Rua de São João 67–69, Angra do Heroísmo, Terceira ▪ (295) 213 729 ▪ Closed Sun
O Forno is the place to indulge in Terceira's famed *bolos Dona Amélia*, sugar-coated cupcakes that are named after Portugal's last queen.

3 **Queijo Vaquinha**
MAP L5 ▪ Canada Pilar 5, Cinco Ribeiras, Terceira ▪ (295) 907 138
Take a guided tour of this cheese factory and sample their renowned *queijo vaquinha* (small cow's cheese).

4 **Mercado Duque de Bragança**
MAP U3 ▪ Rua da Sé, Angra do Heroísmo, Terceira ▪ Closed Sat evening; Sun
This historic farmers' market is worth browsing for fresh fish and handpicked fruits and vegetables.

5 **Açorbordados**
MAP U4 ▪ Rua da Rocha 50, Angra do Heroísmo, Terceira ▪ Closed Sat evening; Sun
This long-established, family-run business is noted for its hand-embroidered towels, curtains and tablemats, woven on site *(see p58)*.

6 **Quinta dos Açores**
MAP N5 ▪ Pico Redondo 149, São Bento, Terceira ▪ (295) 216 213
Wines, fresh meat and dairy produce assorted fruits and vegetables and home-made jams from across the islands are stocked at this impressive indoor deli-style market.

7 **Casa Astória**
MAP P5 ▪ Rua de Jesus 103, Praia da Vitória, Terceira ▪ (295) 512 945
Shop at Astória for authentic mementos such as plasterwork *impérios* – miniature replicas of the Holy Spirit chapels *(see p80)* found all over the islands and especially ornate on Terceira.

8 **Queijadas da Graciosa**
MAP K5 ▪ Canada Nova 34–36, Rochela, Praia (São Mateus), Graciosa ▪ (295) 712 911 ▪ Closed Sun
The cinnamon-flavoured sweet and creamy cakelets are a regional delicacy. Take home a box or two.

9 **Adega e Cooperativa Agrícola da Ilha Graciosa**
Pedras Brancas wines including smooth Angelica Vinho Licoroso and fiery Aguardente Vínica are sold here. Pink garlic and Galia melon produced in the same estate are also stocked *(see p81)*.

10 **Associação de Artesãos da Ilha Graciosa**
Run by volunteers, the arts and crafts cooperative of Graciosa is a joy to discover. The skilled women artisans create exquisitely embroidered tablecloths *(see p81)*.

See map on pp76–7

Outdoor Activities

1 **Diving**
MAP M6 ■ Arraia Divers: www.arraiadivers.com

The Banco D João de Castro seamount off Terceira is considered one of the archipelago's best dive sites (see p25). The *Terceirense* shipwreck is Graciosa's premier dive spot.

2 **Bird-watching**
Gracipescas: www.gracipescas.com.pt

Observe birdlife from rich maritime habitats such as Ilhéu da Praia off Graciosa (see pp78–9). The Cabo da Praia and Ponta das Contendas (see p80) are Terceira's birding hot spots.

3 **Golf**
MAP N5 ■ Clube de Golfe da Ilha Terceira Fajãs da Agualva: www.terceiragolf.com

Several water features challenge accuracy of play on this 18-hole par 72 layout, considered the easiest of the islands' three courses (see p73).

4 **Whale and Dolphin Watching**
MAP V4 ■ Ocean Emotion: www.oceanemotion.pt

Whales can be spotted throughout the summer months, while several species of dolphins stay for winter. The sperm whale is a notable year-round resident (see p17).

5 **Fishing**
Calypso Azores: www.calypsoazores.com

Whether trolling for sawfish, mackerel and barracuda, or bottom fishing from an anchored vessel to catch bream and snapper, the Azorean sea provides an amazing ocean bounty.

6 **Stand Up Paddle (SUP)**
Pristine Azores: www.pristineazores.com

Stand up paddleboard over shallow waters and across spectacular bays while admiring the scenic coastline.

7 **Health and Wellbeing**
MAP K6 ■ Termas do Carapacho, Graciosa

Bathe in hot thermal waters, step under a Vichy shower or limber up in a hydrogymnastics class (see p79).

8 **Caving**
TuriAzores: turiazores.com

On Terceira, visitors can descend to the island's core, Algar do Carvão (see pp30–31). Graciosa lures with its remarkable Furna do Enxofre (see p78). Speleologists should visit Os Montanheiros (see p80).

9 **Horse Riding**
Azoresgo: www.azoresgo.com

The Lusitano is an ideal horse breed on which to explore Terceira's forests. Youngsters will love the miniature donkeys on Graciosa (see p81).

10 **Walking**
ComunicAir: www.comunicair.com

The demanding 40-km (24-mile) circular Grande Rota da Graciosa takes in geosites such as Caldeirinha de Pêro Botelho. Terceira can be hiked using seven official trails.

Hiking on the hills of Terceira

Cafés and Bars

1 Verde Maçã Café
MAP V4 ▪ Rua Direita 111–113, Angra do Heroísmo, Terceira ▪ (295) 218 294

This bar-café is famous for its basalt stone arches and pop-art murals. The menu includes panini and bruschetta, alongside sinful desserts.

2 Hamburgueria do Teatro
MAP U3 ▪ Rua da Esperança 20, Angra do Heroísmo, Terceira ▪ (295) 218 019

The plate-sized burgers land on the table with an audible thud at this cheerful venue. Warm dry weather sees tables arranged on the terrace.

3 A Minha Casa
MAP V4 ▪ Rua Direita 80, Angra do Heroísmo, Terceira ▪ (295) 218 573 ▪ Closed Tue

With its shabby chic decor, a wall festooned with vinyl LP covers and thrift-sale furniture, "My House" is the quirkiest café in town.

4 Birou Bar
MAP U4 ▪ Rua de São João, Angra do Heroísmo, Terceira ▪ (295) 702 180 ▪ Closed Sun

Nip in here for a frappé topped with whipped cream. Meals include shrimp tagliatelle and tuna salad. The mojito is the cocktail of choice (see p55).

The interior of Birou Bar

5 Delman Bar & Lounge
MAP P5 ▪ Rua da Alfândega 22A, Praia da Vitória, Terceira ▪ (961) 836 423

Enjoy petiscos (snacks) at this lunchtime spot while admiring the pleasant waterfront view. The bar is known for its eye-popping gin menu.

6 Garça
MAP P5 ▪ Avenida Álvaro Martins Homem, Praia da Vitória, Terceira ▪ (295) 512 837 ▪ Closed Tue

Patrons come to Garça, established in 1956, for good local cooking and a sports pub atmosphere. There are occasional live-music performances.

7 Pub Bar Vila Sacramento
MAP J5 ▪ Estrada Nova, Santa Cruz da Graciosa, Graciosa ▪ (295) 712 236

Expect a thumping mix of house, Latin and electro at this bar and music club. Parties have previously featured African kizomba dancing (see p55).

8 Snack-Bar O Galeão
MAP J5 ▪ Rua 25 de Abril 30, Santa Cruz da Graciosa, Graciosa ▪ (295) 712 017

Savoury dishes are served with a side of light-hearted banter at this eatery. House specials include caldeirada de peixe (fish casserole) and cabrito estufado (stewed goat).

9 Café e Sabores Félix
MAP K5 ▪ Rua Fontes Pereira de Melo 138, Praia, Graciosa ▪ (295) 732 146

Drop by for some queijadas da Graciosa – cinnamon-flavoured star-shaped tarts filled with deliciously smooth caramel cream.

10 Grafil Coffee Bar
MAP J5 ▪ Largo Conde de Simas 4, Santa Cruz da Graciosa, Graciosa ▪ (295) 712 144

Sip a drink while watching innovative live-music sessions featuring rock and classically trained musicians.

Restaurants

1 Cais de Angra
MAP V4 ■ Marina de Angra do Heroísmo, Terceira ■ (295) 628 458 ■ DA ■ €€

Comfort food meets traditional Portuguese at this lively restaurant. Choose between tender ribs in smoky BBQ sauce, or mushroom risotto. Exotic *caipirinha* cocktails make perfect apéritifs *(see p54)*.

2 O Chico
MAP V4 ■ Rua de São João 7, Angra do Heroísmo, Terceira ■ (295) 333 286 ■ Closed Sun ■ €

Family run and exuding warmth and hospitality, O Chico is a favourite with locals. The menu lists Azorean staples including *alcatra (see p56)*.

Contemporary setting at Aroma

3 Aroma
MAP K5 ■ Graciosa Resort, Porto da Barra, Graciosa ■ (295) 730 500 ■ €€

This contemporary dining space adds a touch of sophistication to the island's culinary scene. Signature dishes honour Azorean gastronomy.

4 Os Moínhos
MAP P6 ■ Rua do Arrabalde, São Sebastião, Terceira ■ (295) 904 508 ■ Closed Tue (in winter) ■ €€

Named for its ancient water wheel, this converted millhouse is the place to enjoy *telha de marisco*, a rich creamy casserole served in earthenware.

5 Ti Choa
MAP L5 ■ Groto do Margarida 1, Serreta, Terceira ■ (295) 906 673 ■ Closed Sun; Tue & Thu lunch ■ €

Dining in this rustic space is like eating in a traditional farmhouse. The decor enhances the rural charm.

6 O Pedro
MAP M4 ■ Caminho do Concelho, Biscoitos, Terceira ■ (961) 434 988 ■ Closed Sun ■ DA ■ €

The eclectic menu at this delightfully ramshackle restaurant features home-style dishes and a decent wine list.

7 Casa de Pasto Bela Vista
MAP P5 ■ Vale Farto 30, nr Praia da Vitória, Terceira ■ (295) 513 424 ■ Closed Wed ■ €€

A stone-clad, country-style interior emphasizes the old-fashioned character of this good-value restaurant.

8 O Cachalote
MAP U3 ■ Rua do Rego 14, Angra do Heroísmo, Terceira ■ (914) 237 459 ■ Closed Sun; Sat lunch ■ €

This hole-in-the-wall eatery is known for its generous steaks, which diners cook to their liking on hot basalt stone.

9 Quinta das Grotas
MAP J5 ■ Caminho das Grotos 28, Ribeirinha, Graciosa ■ (295) 712 334 ■ Closed Mon (in winter) ■ €€

The island food served here includes grilled *mero* (Atlantic goliath grouper) with salad and boiled potatoes.

10 Dolphin Snack Bar
MAP K6 ■ Caminho Carapacho, Carapacho, Graciosa ■ (295) 712 014 ■ €

This eatery is a short walk from the Carapacho Spa *(see p79)*. Specialities are fish and seafood dishes.

See map on pp76–7

TOP10 São Jorge, Pico and Faial Islands

Resembling an emerald shard anchored in an ice-blue sea, São Jorge captivates with its superb hiking trails, many of which take in the famous *fajãs (see p43)*. The island's reputation extends to producing some of the tastiest cheeses in the Azores. Pico, dominated by its enormous volcanic cone, offers some of the world's most rewarding whale watching, while its vineyards are a UNESCO World Heritage Site. As the mid-Atlantic's yachting capital, nearby Faial is proud of its seafaring heritage. The central caldera astounds, but it is the Capelinhos volcano that truly captures the imagination.

Majestic Montanha do Pico

① Montanha do Pico
MAP M3 ■ Casa da Montanha: Caminho Florestal 9, Pico ■ (967) 303 519

Portugal's highest mountain reaches 2,351 m (7,708 ft) above sea level and is emblematic of the Azores' natural wonders. It is possible to ascend Pico independently, but engaging an official guide is strongly recommended.

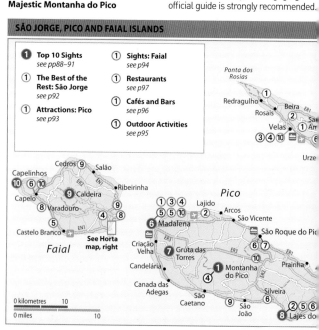

SÃO JORGE, PICO AND FAIAL ISLANDS

Previous pages The striking façade of Império da Caridade in Praia da Vitória, Terceira

Alternatively, conquer the summit as part of a climbing group *(see p95)*. The trailhead begins at the Casa da Montanha – the Mountain House – where climbers need to register.

② Serra do Topo–Fajã da Caldeira de Santo Cristo–Fajã dos Cubres Trail

MAP Q2 ■ Centro de Interpretação da Fajã da Caldeira de Santo Cristo, São Jorge ■ (295) 403 860 ■ Open Apr–Nov: 10am–noon & 1–4pm Sat & Sun (Jun–Sep: Wed–Sun); Dec–Mar: 10am–noon & 1–4pm Sat ■ Adm

Serra do Topo is the departure point for one of the best walks in the Azores. Stunning views take in the Fajã da Caldeira de Santo Cristo lagoon. Once at Caldeira de Santo Cristo, visit the interpretation centre, which offers a fascinating glimpse into the geological and social history of the region. Find out more about the island's *fajãs* – classified by UNESCO as Biosphere Reserves – then continue towards the photogenic Fajã dos Cubres *(see p43)*.

Rich decor of Igreja de Santa Bárbara

③ Igreja de Santa Bárbara

MAP N2 ■ Caminho de Baixa, Manadas, São Jorge

This splendid 18th-century Baroque church is one of the most richly decorated in the Azores, featuring panels of *azulejos* that illustrate the story of Santa Bárbara. The basalt-covered 16th-century font is the only surviving piece of the original church, while the excellent cedarwood ceiling is a rare architectural feature *(see p40)*.

São Jorge, Pico and Faial Islands

4 Complexo Monte de Guia: Casa dos Dabney e Aquário de Porto Pim

Wealthy merchant John Bass Dabney (1766–1826) arrived here from Boston in 1804 and was soon appointed first US consul to the Azores. Whaling and other business interests generated wealth and prestige for the family, and the museum imparts their story. The pairing of the Casa dos Dabney with the Porto Pim Aquarium is convenient for visitors: the same ticket grants entry to the aquarium, which is a holding place for various finned species before they are rehoused in aquariums around the world (see pp26–7).

The brightly coloured Museu do Vinho

CABLE CAPITAL OF THE WORLD

Its mid-Atlantic position made Horta suitable for the anchoring of transatlantic telegraph cables. The first cable was laid in 1893, linking the town with Ponta Delgada and on to Carcavelos, near Lisbon. By the mid-20th century Horta was one of the world's most important cable centres, relaying messages and meteorological observations. The last cable company left in 1969.

5 Museu da Horta

Apart from displaying fig tree pith sculptures (see p61), Horta Museum records the island's artistic, nautical, technological and ethnographic development. The work of José Júlio de Sousa Pinto (1856–1939) is on display: look for his *A Volta dos Barcos* painting. A hall is dedicated to advancements in transatlantic telegraphic communications. The building was a Jesuit College; next door is the Igreja Matriz de São Salvador (see p27).

6 Museu do Vinho

Matchbox vineyards hemmed in by *currais* front this wine museum, which tells Pico's winemaking history through well-illustrated panels. Make sure you play the "Aromas" game, where you match different scents with various fruits and condiments. Later, discover a vintage winepress and other early equipment. Finish up in the tasting room where wines can be sampled and purchased (see p32).

7 Gruta das Torres

MAP L2 ▪ Caminho da Gruta das Torres, Criação Velha, Pico ▪ (924) 403 921 ▪ Open Jun–Sep: 10am–6pm daily; Oct–May: 10am–5pm Tue–Fri, 2–5:30pm Sat ▪ Adm

The largest lava tube in the Azores is a Regional Natural Monument. An astonishing 5,150 m (16,900 ft) in length, this cave is a remarkable volcanic phenomenon. Join a guided tour to walk a 450-m (1,476-ft) section bristling with stalactites, stalagmites and peculiar rock formations.

8 Museu dos Baleeiros

MAP N3 ■ Rua dos Baleeiros 13, Lajes do Pico, Pico ■ (292) 679 340 ■ Open Apr–Sep: 10am–5:30pm Tue–Sun; Oct & Nov: 9.30am–5pm Tue–Sun ■ Adm

The Whalers' Museum is a must-visit for anyone interested in the history of whaling and its social and economic impact on the islands. Before browsing the exhibition, watch the documentary shot in the early 1970s – it perfectly captures the sense of occasion, the drama of the moment and a way of life that by then was in decline (see p39).

9 Caldeira

Faial's enormous crater, 2 km (1 mile) in diameter and 400 m (1,312 ft) deep – is one of the largest in the Azores. The rim, embroidered by cyan- and lilac-hued hydrangeas in summer, is a 7-km (4-mile) nature trail. The trailhead begins at the caldera viewpoint, which also starts the Ten Volcanoes hike (see p29).

10 Capelinhos

A compulsory stop on any Faial itinerary, Capelinhos is synonymous with the events of 1957 and 1958 when earth tremors and volcanic eruptions struck the area. Blanketed with lava and ash, the terrain resembles a lunar landscape. The lighthouse, Farol dos Capelinhos, survived the seismic onslaught. It stands over a subterranean, futuristic-looking interpretative centre. Here the Capelinhos volcano phenomenon and volcanology is explained using film, holographic and interactive media (see pp28–9).

Capelinhos' lunar-style landscape

A DAY EXPLORING PICO

▶ MORNING

Start your day with breakfast at Caffe 5 in Madalena (see p96), then follow the road signs to Criação Velha. If you're visiting during the summer and want to explore the Gruta das Torres, the first guided tour of the cave commences at 10:30am. A leisurely drive along the ER-1-2 takes in the island's picturesque south coast, passing villages such as Candelária and São Caetano. To your left, the mighty Montanha do Pico is ever present, and its form changes dramatically as you head towards Lajes do Pico (see p93), one of the most popular destinations on the island. Take time to browse the fantastic Museu dos Baleeiros and then enjoy a light lunch at Pastelaria Aromas & Sabores (see p96).

AFTERNOON

Double back out of Lajes to Ribeira do Cabo where the EN-3 will take you up to the mountains. This is an inspiring drive, where at 700 m (2,296 ft) the landscape is all hills and pastureland. As you see a road sign to Madalena on your left, turn for a quick diversion to the enchanting Lagoa do Capitão (see p93). Return to the EN-3 and descend to São Roque do Pico. The Museu da Indústria Baleeira (see p93) is worth visiting before continuing to Santa Luzia where you take the road to Pico's UNESCO-protected vineyards (see pp32–3). Stop here to visit the old distillery, adega and the interpretive centre (closed Oct–May: Mon) where you can stock up on some fabulous wines before your journey back to Madalena.

See map on pp88–9 ←

The Best of the Rest: São Jorge

1 Parque Florestal das Sete Fontes

MAP M1

The Seven Fountains recreational forest reserve is perfect for picnics and can be combined with a trip to Ponta dos Rosais, at the island's western tip.

Parque Florestal das Sete Fontes

2 Uniqueijo

MAP N1 ▪ Beira ▪ (295) 438 274 ▪ Tours: 10am–4pm Mon–Fri ▪ Adm

São Jorge's rich cheeses, regarded as the best in the Azores, are made here. Call ahead for a guided tour (see p59).

3 Casa do Parque de São Jorge

MAP P1 ▪ Estrada Regional, Norte Grande ▪ Open Jun–Sep: 10am–6pm daily; Oct–May: 10am–5pm Mon–Fri, 2–5:30pm Sat

The Caldeirinhas-Norte Grande trail (see p46) takes hikers past the island's Natural Park visitor's centre.

4 Grutas do Algar do Montoso

MAP N2

The little explored Montoso caves entice with the promise of a descent into the island's volcanic belly (see p95).

5 Topo and Ilhéu do Topo

MAP R3

São Jorge's first settlers landed at this isolated far eastern point. There is a lighthouse on the Topo islet, which is a protected sanctuary for birds.

6 Cooperativa de Artesanato Nossa Senhora da Encarnação

MAP N2 ▪ Ribeira do Nabo, nr Urzelina ▪ (295) 414 296 ▪ 9am–5pm daily

Local women create woven items, ceramics, basalt carvings and jams (see p60) at this handicraft cooperative.

7 Urzelina

MAP N2

In 1808 volcanic lava engulfed the entire village except the clock tower, which still remains, marked by a plaque and a solidified lava chunk.

8 Calheta

MAP P2 ▪ Museum: Rua José Azevedo da Cunha ▪ (295) 416 323 ▪ Open summer: 10am–5:30pm Tue–Sun; winter: 9:30am–5pm Tue–Sun ▪ Adm

The island's second-largest town is proud of its seafaring heritage. The Museu Francisco de Lacerda (see p37) is worth investigating.

9 Casa de Artesanato Nunes

MAP Q2 ▪ Fajã do Vimes ▪ (295) 416 717

Traditional handmade woollen bedspreads are crafted at this workshop. Nearby is Café Nunes (see p96), famous for its homegrown coffee.

10 Velas

MAP N1

From the harbour, stroll under the 18th-century gateway, Portão do Mar. The parish church watches over a web of cobbled streets.

Town square, Velas

Attractions: Pico

A scenic view of the harbour and the pretty town of Madalena

1 Madalena
MAP L2

The first port of call on the island, Madalena wins visitors over with its tidy harbour, 16th-century Igreja de Santa Maria Madalena and the acclaimed Museu do Vinho (see p90).

2 Paisagem da Cultura da Vinha da Ilha do Pico

UNESCO has declared Pico's vineyards a testimony to the island's cultural tradition. The area is worthy of its World Heritage status (see pp32–3).

3 Cooperativa Vitivinícola
MAP L2 ■ Avenida Padre Nunes da Rosa, Madalena ■ (292) 622 262 ■ Open 8am–5pm Mon–Fri ■ Adm

Established in 1949, this respected winery creates Frei Gigante, Terras de Lava and Basalto, among other quality reds and whites (see p32).

4 Museu dos Cachalotes e Lulas
MAP L2 ■ Avenida Machado Serpa, Madalena ■ Open Jun–Sep: 10am–5:30pm Tue–Fri, 1–5pm Sat & Sun; Oct–May: 9am–5pm Mon–Fri ■ Adm

Cephalopods meet cetaceans at this Museum of Sperm Whales and Squids. The exhibition is highly educational.

5 Lajes do Pico
MAP N3

This town is where whale watching began. The Museu dos Baleeiros (see p91) chronicles the timeline.

6 Museu da Indústria Baleeira
MAP N2 ■ Rua do Poço, Cais do Poço, São Roque do Pico ■ (292) 642 096 ■ Open summer: 10am–5:30pm Tue–Sun; winter: 9:30am–5pm Tue–Sun ■ Adm (free on Sun)

A former whaling factory is now an engaging museum, where disused machinery still fires the imagination.

7 Escola Regional de Artesanato
MAP P3 ■ Rua Barão Manuel Nunes Melo 9, Santo Amaro ■ (914) 084 522 ■ Open 9am–5pm Mon–Fri

The island's traditional handicrafts are showcased in this workshop and museum. Visitors can buy handmade mementos here (see p60–61).

8 Calheta do Nesquim Trail
MAP Q3

This circular walk provides an added dimension to sightseeing in Calheta do Nesquim. The village was once a thriving whaling community.

9 Mistérios de São João
MAP M3

Leisure activities are on offer at this forest reserve, which was shaped by a volcanic eruption in 1718.

10 Lagoa do Capitão Trail
MAP N2

On a clear day Montanha do Pico (see p88–9) is reflected in the "Captain's Lake", where this walk begins.

See map on pp88–9 ←

Sights: Faial

1 Fábrica da Baleia de Porto Pim

MAP T4 ▪ Monte da Guia, Horta ▪ (292) 292 140 ▪ Open 1 Apr–14 Jun & 16 Sep–31 Oct: 9:30am–4:30pm Mon–Fri, 2–5:30pm Sat & Sun; 15 Jun–15 Sep: 10am–6pm daily; Nov–Mar: 9am–5:30pm Mon–Fri ▪ Adm

This former whaling station shows how industrial the pursuit of whales was in the past. Also housed here is the Marine Virtual Interpretation Centre.

2 Monte da Guia

MAP J3 ▪ Horta

This promontory offers fine views over Horta. A road leads to a 17th-century chapel dedicated to Senhora da Guia. The summit is closed to visitors.

3 Oceaneye

MAP J3 ▪ Rua Doutor Manuel Garcia Monteiro, Horta ▪ (966) 140 608 ▪ Timings depend on weather conditions (call ahead) ▪ Adm

The glass-bottomed *Ana G* plies the shallows off Faial and Pico allowing passengers a clear view of the seabed. The trip showcases the Azores' astonishing marine biodiversity.

4 Jardim Botânico do Faial

Set in the grounds of the Quinta de São Lourenço, this botanic garden displays endemic plants of the Azores. Highlights include an orchid garden. Visitors can also opt for guided tours (see p27).

5 Lombega–Morro de Castelo Branco Trail

MAP H3 ▪ Lombega

Ramble out of Lombega village where this walk starts. The route brings hikers up to the Castelo Branco headland, where many seabirds reside.

6 Escola de Artesanato do Capelo

MAP G2 ▪ Alto dos Cavacos, nr Capelo ▪ (292) 945 027

This school promotes local artists who can be observed creating traditional handicrafts. Terceiran embroidery is especially valued, but there are many items worth buying (see pp60–61).

7 Horta

Vibrant Horta exudes nautical bonhomie, as bobbing yachts line the marina and the lanes echo foreign tongues. Best explored on foot, Faial's only town reveals its centuries-old cultural heritage (see pp26–7).

A windmill at Ponta da Espalamaca

8 Ponta da Espalamaca

MAP K3 ▪ Espalamaca

Much photographed, the windmills dotting Espalamaca Point add colour with their red *casotas* (bonnets) topping the basalt stone bases. The outline of Pico provides a theatrical backdrop.

9 Praia do Almoxarife

MAP K3 ▪ Facho

Famed for its black sand beach – a popular summer destination – the region around Almoxarife is also noted for its picturesque valley, with meadows rolling towards the sea.

10 Parque Florestal do Capelo

MAP G2 ▪ Capelo

A demanding mountain bike trail threads its way under the canopy of Capelo's recreational forest reserve. Hikers can explore at a slower pace.

Outdoor Activities

1 Vineyard Tours
Visit Pico: www.picothe azores.com

Visit wineries, find out more about the island's grape varieties and marvel at the UNESCO-recognized vineyards in one of the world's most unusual wine regions *(see pp32–3)*.

2 Whale and Dolphin Watching
MAP N3 ▪ Horta Cetáceos: www. hortacetaceos.com

Pico and Faial are the best islands for whale observation and study. The azure ocean is also a playground for frisky dolphins *(see pp16–17)*.

3 Horse Riding
Pátio: www.patio.pt

Atop obedient Portuguese Lusitano and Cruzado horses, follow ancient paths through historic villages, verdant forests and windblown cliffs.

4 Climbing Pico
MAP M3 ▪ Tripix Azores: www. tripixazores.com

Intrepid travellers with lots of energy and a head for heights can scale the summit of Portugal's highest mountain *(see pp88–9)*. Hiring an official guide is recommended.

5 Nature Hikes and Walks
Discover Experience Azores: www.discoverexperienceazores.com

Much of São Jorge can only be reached on foot, including a number of fajãs *(see p43)* dotting the island.

Hiking in the São Jorge mountains

Regatta between Faial and Pico

6 Sailing
MAP T3 ▪ Sea & Sail Azores: seasailazores.com

Hoist the sails and chart a course out of Horta to navigate the classic *triângulo* – the triangular island-hop between Faial, Pico and São Jorge.

7 Diving
MAP T3 ▪ DiveAzores: dive azores.net

Chilean devil rays frequent the Banco Princesa Alice seamount *(see p25)*, a dive spot equidistant from Pico and Faial. The Gruta dos Camarões, near Horta, is famed for Narwal shrimps.

8 Kayaking
Naturfactor: www.natur factor.com

Paddling Pico's coastline of bays, caves and basalt rock formations is an invigorating pastime.

9 Mountain Biking
Casa d'Avilas: www.casa davilas.com

Whether negotiating mountain paths or riding through woodlands, pro-pelling a mountain bike off the beaten track is one of the most exhilarating ways of taking in island scenery.

10 Caving and Geotourism
Aventour – Azores Adventures: www.aventour.pt

Magical and mysterious, the caves and grottoes honeycombed deep beneath the ground include the immense Algar do Montoso *(see p92)*.

See map on pp88–9

Cafés and Bars

① Café Nunes
MAP Q2 ▪ Fajã dos Vimes, São Jorge ▪ (295) 416 717

It is a long way to go for coffee, but what is poured is totally unique. They make Arabica coffee from beans grown in the village, the only place in Europe where coffee is cultivated.

Diners at Peter Café Sport

② Peter Café Sport
MAP T3 ▪ Rua José Azevedo 9, Horta, Faial ▪ (292) 292 327

Opt for steak and grilled sardines, along with one of Peter's famous cocktails. The fascinating Museu de Scrimshaw is upstairs (see p55).

③ Café Açor
MAP N1 ▪ Rua da Matriz 41, Velas, São Jorge ▪ (295) 432 463

Centrally located, this café overlooks the square and its church. Families flock to the terrace in summer.

④ Koppus Bar
MAP N1 ▪ Avenida 19 de Outubro, Velas, São Jorge ▪ (295) 098 507 ▪ Closed Mon

Funky DJ sets, live bands and the glamorous "Ladies' Nite" entice clubbers to this crowd-puller (see p55).

⑤ Caffe 5
MAP L2 ▪ Rua Carlos Dabney 5, Madalena, Pico ▪ (292) 623 970 ▪ Closed Sun

Vegetarians will appreciate the menu at this breezy snack bar, known for its creative and inexpensive food. The Guinness, Erdinger and Budweiser will tempt beer drinkers.

⑥ Pastelaria Aromas & Sabores
MAP N3 ▪ Rua Capitão Mor G.G. Madruga, Lajes do Pico, Pico ▪ (292) 672 877 ▪ Closed Sun

Sample the bakery's very own *bolo baleeiro* (see p59) or enjoy one of their sweet liqueurs. A convenient breakfast venue and a favoured lunch spot for locals.

⑦ Bar Esplanade Clube Naval
MAP N2 ▪ Praceta dos Baleeiros, São Roque, Pico ▪ (292) 642 105

Handy for the São Jorge ferry, the navy club's dockside café-bar is good for a quick snack. It also makes a good coffee stop after visiting the Museu da Indústria Baleeira (see p93).

⑧ Casa de Chá e Bar
MAP S2 ▪ Rua de São João 38A, Horta, Faial ▪ (292) 700 053 ▪ Closed Wed

A perfect place to enjoy tea and cake in a serene garden setting, the elegant Tea House also tempts with healthy snacks plus coffee, wines and beers. The rooftop terrace is a blissful retreat.

⑨ Taberna de Pim
MAP T4 ▪ Rua Nova 3, Horta ▪ (934) 108 720 ▪ Closed Oct–Mar

This waterfront bistro offers a broad view of Horta's old harbour. Arrive late afternoon, order a chilled white wine and let the world catch up. If it is not busy, try the food.

⑩ Café Volga
MAP T3 ▪ Praça Infante Dom Henrique 16, Horta, Faial ▪ (292) 292 347

There is a pleasing lack of ceremony at this informal eatery, making it the ideal choice for a simple snack with no trimmings. Order a *bifana* (steak sandwich) and blend in with the locals.

Restaurants

1 Fornos de Lava
MAP N1 ■ Travessa de São Tiago 46, Santo Amaro, São Jorge ■ (295) 432 415 ■ Closed 22 Dec–1 Jan ■ €€

The kitchen leans towards country fare but the menu also lists creative seafood dishes *(see p55)*.

2 Almicar
MAP P1 ■ Fajã do Ouvidor, São Jorge ■ (295) 417 448 ■ Closed Tue ■ €€

Sitting on the edge of the harbour is this cheerful little eatery whose speciality is *ameijoas* (clams).

3 Genuíno
MAP S4 ■ Areinha Velha 9, Angustias, Horta, Faial ■ (292) 701 542 ■ Closed Wed; all of Jan ■ €€

Brilliantly prepared fish and seafood, a notable wine list and lovely views of Porto Pim place Genuíno among the Azores' best restaurants *(see p54)*.

4 Canto da Doca
MAP T3 ■ Rua Nova, Horta, Faial ■ (292) 292 444 ■ €

Order your meat or seafood, then cook it yourself on a hot slab of lava stone.

5 Cella Bar
MAP L2 ■ Lugar da Barca, nr Madalena, Pico ■ (292) 623 654 ■ €€

The cursive, wooden skin of this bar-restaurant is an award-winning

modern design statement. The menu is creative, and the wine list second to none. Unbeatable views *(see p55)*.

6 Fonte Cuisine
MAP N3 ■ Aldeia da Fonte, Caminho de Baixo, Silveira, Pico ■ (292) 679 500 ■ €€

Enjoy a romantic dinner amid gardens overlooking a secluded bay. The cuisine honours Portuguese culinary tradition with international flourishes.

7 Ponta da Ilha
MAP Q3 ■ Caminho de Baixo, Manhenha, Pico ■ (292) 666 708 ■ €

Located at the eastern tip of Pico, this eatery is run by the Artisanal Fisheries Ship Owners Association. Seafood specialities include grilled fish kebabs.

8 Vista da Baía
MAP G2 ■ Varadouro, nr Capelo, Faial ■ (292) 945 140 ■ Open in summer only ■ €

This is the place to visit for home-style chicken, grilled to perfection. Enjoy it with hot garlic bread and a cold beer.

9 O Esconderijo
MAP J1 ■ Rua Janalves 3, Cedros, Faial ■ (292) 946 505 ■ Open 6–9pm Wed–Mon dinner only (Fri–Sun in winter) ■ €€

Come here for inventive home-made vegetarian fare served in a country cottage-style environment.

10 Ancoradouro
MAP L2 ■ Rua Rodrigo Guerra 7, Madalena, Pico ■ (292) 623 490 ■ Closed Mon ■ Dis. access ■ €€

A picturesque waterfront location near the island's vineyards *(see pp32–3)* enhances the appeal of this noted seafood eatery *(see p55)*.

The striking façade of Cella Bar

See map on pp88–9

🔟 Flores and Corvo Islands

As the westernmost island of the Azores, Flores also anchored at the western extremity of Europe. Peaceful and remote, the island is dotted with lakes and waterfalls, and awash with hydrangeas in summer, their pinkish-lilac hue colouring the landscape. Flores also boasts spectacular hiking trails that wind along coastal cliffs. Neighbouring Corvo is the archipelago's smallest island, a gem moored in isolated splendour. This charming destination is shaped around an awe-inspiring, ancient caldera. These two islands are paired as UNESCO Biosphere Reserves, thanks to their diverse and pristine habitats.

Cascata da Ribeira Grande

FLORES AND CORVO ISLANDS

Flores

- Ponta de Albarnaz
- Ponta Delgada
- • Ponta Delgada
- Ilhéu da Maria Vaz
- ④ Lajedo–Fajã Grande–Ponta Delgada Trail
- ⑥
- Ponta Ruiva
- △ Caldeirinha 753m
- Cedros
- Ponta da Fajã
- △ Morro Alto 911m
- ③⑥⑦
- ①③⑦⑧⑤⑥⑦⑨ Santa Cruz das Flores
- ⑥ Fajã Grande
- ⑧ Sete Lagoas
- Fajãzinha ⑤
- ① Cascata da Ribeira Grande
- △ Pico do Touro 671m
- Caveira
- ② Gruta dos Enxaréus
- Mosteiro •
- Rocha dos Bordões ⑩
- △ Caldeira Funda
- • Lomba
- Lajedo •
- Fazenda das Lajes
- △ Picarneiro 548m
- ④
- Praia da Calheta
- Lajes das Flores
- Ponta da Rocha Alta

0 kilometres 3
0 miles 3

Corvo

- Serão Alto 666m
- ⑤ Caldeirão
- Morro dos Homens 718m
- ②⑨⑩④⑩
- ⑨ Vila do Corvo

0 km 1
0 miles 1

①	**Top 10 Sights** see pp99–101
①	**Places to Eat and Drink** see p103
①	**Outdoor Activities** see p102

1 Cascata da Ribeira Grande

MAP Q6 ▪ Fajãzinha, Flores

Plunging hundreds of metres to roar through a natural amphitheatre of mountain greenery, the Ribeira Grande waterfall is a treat for eyes and ears. The tumbling river nourishes dozens of smaller crystalline waterfalls that plummet into lakes and ponds, including the natural lagoon, Poço do Bacalhau, or the "Codfish Pool".

Museu da Fábrica da Baleia do Boqueirão

2 Gruta dos Enxaréus

MAP R6 ▪ Flores

Accessible by boat and only visible from the sea, this partly submerged cavern is 50 m (164 ft) long and 25 m (82 ft) wide. Local legend suggests that the cave served as a hideout for pirates and smugglers. Modern-day treasure hunters can visit the grotto by joining an ocean-going excursion that also seeks out other caves and rock formations *(see p102).*

3 Museu da Fábrica da Baleia do Boqueirão

MAP R5 ▪ Rua do Boqueirão, Santa Cruz das Flores, Flores ▪ (292) 542 932 ▪ Open Jun–Sep: 9am–5:30pm Mon–Fri, 2–5:30pm Sat & Sun; Oct–May: 9am–12:30pm & 2–5:30pm Mon–Fri, 2–5:30pm Sun ▪ Adm

The old Boqueirão whaling station is now an excellent museum that presents the story of whaling in the Azores. Dating from the early 1940s, this was one of the largest factories of its kind and operated for over 30 years. The factory floor houses original equipment and machinery, while upstairs an interactive exhibition traces the development of the industry.

4 Lajedo–Fajã Grande– Ponta Delgada Trail

MAP Q5 ▪ Flores

The Flores west coast walk stretches 22 km (14 miles) along Europe's westernmost coastline. It is an equally exhilarating hiking challenge whether starting from Lajedo or following a reverse itinerary out of Ponta Delgada. Along the way, look out for the landmark Rocha dos Bordões *(see p101)* in the south and, in the north, the Ilhéu de Monchique, the most western point of Europe. Bird-watchers should note that the largest European colonies of roseate tern nest on these islets *(see p47).*

Coastal landscape at Fajã Grande

Twin lakes encircled by the Caldeirão, the ancient volcanic crater

(5) Caldeirão
MAP R4 ■ Corvo

A profound sense of peace can be experienced when peering into the basin of this huge crater, its allure magnified by the remote location. This is a fertile habitat for American and European migratory birds during autumn, when the island welcomes ornithologists from around the world. Follow the well-signed trail along the rim and down through pastures to the water's edge (see p43).

AUTUMN MIGRATION ON CORVO

At the very edge of the Western Palearctic, Corvo is ideally positioned as a landing stage for the autumn migration of Nearctic waders and wildfowl – North American vagrants that number a spectacular variety of rare species. Adding lustre is the high incidence of Nearctic landbirds. Among those recorded by bird-watchers are white-rumped sandpipers, rose-breasted grosbeaks and laughing gulls. There has even been a yellow-billed cuckoo (above) sighting at Vila do Corvo.

---

(6) Museu das Flores
MAP R5 ■ Edifício do Convento de São Boaventura, Santa Cruz das Flores, Flores ■ (292) 592 159 ■ Open 9am–12:30pm & 2–5:30pm Mon–Fri ■ Adm

Its tranquil setting in the cloisters of a former 17th-century Franciscan convent encourages visitors to linger in this ethnographic museum. The island's whaling heritage is reflected in the display of scrimshaw (see p60), while the sacred art leads visitors to the adjoining church. The nearby 17th-century Casa Museu Pimental de Mesquita is believed to be the oldest home on the island (see p38).

(7) Centro de Interpretação Ambiental do Boqueirão
MAP R5 ■ Rua do Boqueirão 2A, Santa Cruz das Flores, Flores ■ (292) 542 447 ■ Open Jun–Sep: 9am–5:30pm Mon–Fri, 2–5:30pm Sat & Sun; Oct–May: 9am–12:30pm & 2–5:30pm Mon–Fri, 2–5:30pm Sun ■ Guided tours

Housed underground in former whale oil storage tanks, the Boqueirão Environmental Interpretation Centre features a series of exhibition rooms, each highlighting an aspect of the island's biodiversity. There is an area dedicated to the region's resident and migratory birds, and a hall showcasing the different species of cetaceans seen off the Azores (see pp16–17). The highlight is the imaginary "Dive to the Depths" exhibit to discover the sea life drawn to cauldron-like subterranean hydrothermal vents.

⑧ Sete Lagoas
MAP Q6 ■ Flores

Seven lakes of differing size and appearance make up Flores' stunning "lake district". Each lake is worth seeing, although Lagoa Funda merits special mention for its captivating beauty. Nearby Lagoa Rasa is smaller but equally serene, as is Lomba. The cluster of Comprida, Seca, Branca and Caldeira Funda can be hiked. With a depth of 108 m (354 ft), Caldeira Funda is the deepest.

⑨ Centro de Interpretação Ambiental e Cultural
MAP Q4 ■ Canada do Graciosa, Vila do Corvo, Corvo ■ (292) 596 051 ■ Open Jun–Sep: 10am–1pm & 2–6pm daily; Oct–May: 10am–5pm Tue–Fri, 2–5:30pm Sat

Underlining the island's UNESCO Biosphere Reserve status is this cultural and environmental interpretative centre. Visitors can learn about Corvo's cultural attractions and environmental projects, including the wild birds recovery centre (see p102).

⑩ Rocha dos Bordões
MAP Q6 ■ Mosteiro, Flores

The Bordões outcrop is a spectacular geological phenomenon and a superb example of columnar jointing. The most rewarding time to admire the rock is late afternoon on a clear day when it appears as if coated in honey. Look for the *miradouro* (viewpoint) on the road between Lajedo and Mosteiro (see p43).

Rocha dos Bordões

A DAY EXPLORING FLORES

▶ **MORNING**

Start the day the Portuguese way with a *galão* – a large glass of hot milk with a dash of coffee – and a *tosta mista* (toasted cheese and ham sandwich) at **Lucino's** (see p103) in Santa Cruz das Flores. The drive south on the ER-1 briefly skirts the coast. Turn inland on the ER-2 for the high country, passing the Pico da Casinda lookout. Carry on until the Cruzeiro Padre Alfredo crossroads where you will see signs for the **Comprida** and **Funda** lakes. The track is narrow but suitable for vehicles. After absorbing the fabulous scenery turn back and continue on the ER-2 towards Mosteiro. You will soon have the option of turning right for **Fajã Grande** (see p99), worth a detour for the dramatic coastline. Stop for a coffee and some fresh sea air at **Jonah's Snack Bar** (see p103). Then, double back and carry on driving south. Pull up next to the *miradouro* overlooking the amazing **Rocha dos Bordões** on your left. Afterwards, carry on to Lajes das Flores and pause for lunch and to explore the harbour.

AFTERNOON

A leisurely drive north out of Lajes will introduce you to the island's picturesque east coast. The meandering route snakes past scenic Fazenda das Lajes and two watermills before meeting the village of Lomba. Eventually you come to Caveira with its sweeping views of Santa Cruz, just 10 minutes away. There may still be time to visit the **Museu das Flores**.

See map on p98 ←

Outdoor Activities

① Canyoning and Cascading
WestCanyon: www.west
canyon.pt

Landscaped with peaks, gullies, gorges, chasms and some of the highest waterfalls in the Azores, Flores is the archipelago's premier destination for these adrenaline-fuelled pastimes *(see p51)*.

② Diving
Flores Dive Center: www.
floresdivecenter.com

Famed for the abundance of dusky grouper, the Caneiro dos Meros dive site *(see p25)* off Vila do Corvo is the only voluntary marine reserve in the Azores. Those diving off Flores can explore caves such as Gruta do Galo and Gruta dos Enxaréus *(see p99)*.

③ Bird-watching
SPEA: www.spea.pt

Resident species on the island include wood-cocks, canaries and blackcaps, but during the autumn migration North American birds such as blue-winged teals and ruby-crowned kinglets are sighted. Corvo Biological Reserve attracts Cory's shearwaters in summer *(see p53)*.

Ruby-crowned kinglet

④ Centro de Reabilitação de Aves Selvagens do Corvo
MAP R4 ■ Canada do Graciosa, Vila do Corvo, Corvo ■ (292) 596 051

The Wild Birds Recovery Centre is tasked with the rehabilitation of sick and injured birds. This unique facility can be visited by appointment.

⑤ Flores Boat Tours
MAP R5 ■ Hotel Ocidental: www.hotelocidental.com

Skirting the island's scenic coastline by boat reveals outcrops of twisted rock, islets teeming with terns and shearwaters, and mysterious grottoes.

The scenic west coast of Flores

⑥ Trekking
MAP Q5 ■ WestCanyon: www.
westcanyon.pt

Trekking the west coast of Flores in summer means ambling through fields walled with bright hydrangeas. This 500-year-old footpath offers a varied and scenic hike *(see p99)*.

⑦ Fishing
MAP R5 ■ Zagaia Flores: www.
zagaiaflores.pt

Try your luck spinning or jigging to lure yellowmouth barracuda and other denizens of the deep.

⑧ Tours of Flores
Sílvio Medina: www.toursof
flores.com

Sightseeing the island by minivan taxi allows visitors to sit back as a driver-guide steers in the right direction.

⑨ Excursions to Corvo
MAP R5 ■ Passeios Turísticos: (917) 918 964/(964) 220 645

Jump aboard a rigid inflatable for a thrill-a-minute boat ride to neigh-bouring Corvo. The itinerary navigates selected areas of the coastline.

⑩ Lacticorvo
MAP R4 ■ Caminho da Horta Funda, Vila do Corvo, Corvo ■ (292) 596 005 ■ Open 9am–noon & 1:30–5pm Mon–Fri

Queijo do Corvo (Corvo cheese), an island delicacy, is produced at this artisan dairy. Tour the factory and sample the cheeses before buying.

Places to Eat and Drink

1 Das Flores Café & Wine
MAP R5 ▪ Aeroporto, Santa Cruz das Flores, Flores ▪ (910) 320 492 ▪ €

Locally sourced ingredients flavour a menu of light meals and desserts. Murals by local artists line the walls.

2 Irmãos Metralha
MAP R4 ▪ Rua Joaquim Pedro Coelho, Vila do Corvo, Corvo ▪ (292) 596 141 ▪ Closed mid-Dec–first week in Jan ▪ €

A characterful, hole-in-the-wall bar that serves light snacks during the day.

3 Lucino's
MAP R5 ▪ Largo 25 de Abril, Santa Cruz das Flores, Flores ▪ (292) 592 633 ▪ €

This centrally located café-bar is a good breakfast stop for pies, cakes and sandwiches (see p55).

4 Casa do Rei
MAP R6 ▪ Rua Peixoto Pimentel 33, Lajes das Flores, Flores ▪ (292) 593 262 ▪ Closed lunch; Tue (Oct–Apr) ▪ €

Rustic chic describes this restaurant. The kitchen features Portuguese cuisine with meat and fish dishes.

A selection of dishes at Casa do Rei

5 Pôr do Sol
MAP Q6 ▪ Fajãzinha, Flores ▪ (292) 552 075 ▪ Closed Mon (in summer); Mon–Fri (Sep–Apr) ▪ €€

Try the *morcela* (black pudding) with sweet yam appetizer at this traditional farmhouse eatery. Its coastal location is why the place also serves seaweed patties, a local delicacy (see p54).

6 Jonah's Snack Bar
MAP Q6 ▪ Rua Senador André de Freitas 20, Fajã Grande, Flores ▪ (292) 552 043 ▪ Closed Dec ▪ €

This homely eatery offers wholesome island cuisine and snacks to go – handy if hiking the west coast (see p47).

7 O Moleiro
MAP R5 ▪ Zona Industrial do Boqueirão, Santa Cruz das Flores, Flores ▪ (911) 047 276 ▪ Closed mid-Dec–first week in Jan ▪ €

Look past the industrial location; the menu here is value for money. The *cherne* (wreckfish) is recommended.

8 Amanhecer
MAP R5 ▪ Rua Doutor Armas da Silveira 21, Santa Cruz das Flores, Flores ▪ (292) 542 111 ▪ Closed Mon; Sun dinner ▪ €

Portugal meets India with dishes such as pan-fried parrotfish with garam masala. The chef is happy to prepare vegetarian meals too.

9 A Traineira
MAP R4 ▪ Rua da Matriz, Vila do Corvo, Corvo ▪ (292) 596 088 ▪ Closed Sun; 10 Dec–10 Jan ▪ €

Summer sees a daily-changing menu. Fish dishes include *tortilha de atum*, or Spanish-style tuna (see p54).

10 O Caldeirão
MAP R4 ▪ Caminho dos Moinhos, Vila do Corvo, Corvo ▪ (918) 444 945 ▪ Closed Wed ▪ €

The unpretentious atmosphere at this eatery is refreshing. Portions are generous and well priced.

See map on p98

Streetsmart

A scenic path along the mountains
overlooking the coast of São Miguel

Getting To and Around the Azores

Arriving by Air

Airports serve all nine islands of the Azores. **João Paulo II Airport** on São Miguel is located 3 km (2 miles) west of Ponta Delgada and is operated by **Aeroportas de Portugal**. Most international flights arrive and depart from here. **Lajes Airport** on Terceira is the Azores' second-busiest airport.

There are daily flights from most major cities in Europe and the US to Lisbon, which connect to **Horta Airport** on Faial, as well as the airports on São Miguel and Terceira.

There are daily direct flights from Lisbon's Humberto Delgado International Airport to Ponta Delgada with **SATA**, which also flies daily out of Porto, with a Wednesday flight to Lajes.

TAP Air Portugal flies from Lisbon and Porto to Ponta Delgada and Lajes on a daily basis. Low-cost carriers **easyJet** and **Ryanair** also fly direct from Lisbon to Ponta Delgada. In addition, Ryanair operates direct flights out of Lisbon and Porto to Lajes.

SATA has direct flights from Boston and Toronto to Ponta Delgada and Terceira. It is represented by **Azores Express** in the US, and by **SATA Express** in Canada.

Arriving by Sea

The **Portas do Mar** maritime terminal at Ponta Delgada is the first port of call for visitors arriving at São Miguel by cruise ship and interisland ferries. The facility also extends to a recreational marina operated by **Azores Marinas**, which provides berths for over 400 boats.

On Horta the **Porto da Horta** cruise ship terminal and commercial quay is located 1 km (half a mile) northeast of the town centre. The marina, the most popular in the Azores for transatlantic yachts, is sited along the esplanade.

Terceira's cruise port facility is at **Praia da Vitória** on the western coast of the island, 20 km (12 miles) from Angra do Heroísmo.

Besides the marinas at Ponta Delgada, Horta and Praia da Vitória, there are also smaller facilities at Angra do Heroísmo, Vila do Porto, Madalena, Velas and Lajes do Pico.

Island-hopping by Air

All nine islands are linked by SATA, which operates scheduled flights around the archipelago. Flights should be booked well in advance during summer. Adverse weather can disrupt timetables, so for extensive island-hopping, insure against delays. Most flights operating between each island take about 30 to 40 minutes, except São Miguel to Flores, which takes 80 minutes. With an international SATA air ticket visitors can take advantage of an online interisland routing service and receive a discount on interisland fares.

Island-hopping by Sea

A network of ferries operated by **Atlanticoline** linking all the islands allows visitors to explore the archipelago by sea.

Throughout the year there are several daily sailings between Horta and Pico by passenger and car ferries. Between April and September there is a daily Horta–Velas service via Pico and some via São Roque. Pico, Faial and São Jorge are closely clustered – the so-called "triangle" – making it possible to plan your own island-hopping itineraries between the three islands. A special three-in-one ticket is issued by **Triangle The Azores**. There are also seasonal services between Faial, Pico and São Jorge to Angra do Heroísmo. Less frequent are sailings between São Miguel and Santa Maria and the Central Group, including Graciosa, and Flores, in the Western Group. However, a regular operation exists between Flores and Corvo.

Atlanticoline issues Açores 4 tickets that offer concessions, including discounts for families, students and passengers with limited mobility.

Travelling by Bus

Travelling the islands by public transport requires patience and flexibility. Many of the routes are designed for locals and scheduled around working hours, which might be incovenient for tourists. There are no services on Corvo. **Transportes Açores** publishes a list of services on each island, their routes and schedules, available online for download.

The aerobus operated by **UTC** shuttles passengers from São Miguel's João Paulo II Airport to Ponta Delgada, stopping at selected hotels, hostels and guesthouses. Visitors can buy a round-trip ticket in the arrivals hall.

São Miguel offers the most frequent and extensive bus services, allowing visitors to travel out early from Ponta Delgada and spend a day's sightseeing in places such as Sete Cidades, Ribeira Grande, Nordeste and Furnas. There are three private

bus companies: Auto Viação Micaelense, CRP – Caetano, Raposo e Pereiras, and Varela e Companhia. Timetables are available from the tourist office or online at **S. Miguel Transportes**.

Travelling by Taxi

Taxis in the Azores are numerous and relatively inexpensive. Trips are usually metered, although there are fixed charges for certain routes. On occasion, drivers are willing to negotiate a rate. Most tourist offices have lists of local taxi operators, along with their telephone numbers and approximate fees. An island tour by taxi is a popular sightseeing option. Taxis are also a useful way of accessing walks. Many private

taxi operators such as **Azorean Tours** offer full- or half-day programmes following a fixed itinerary.

Travelling by Car

The easiest and most reliable way to get around the islands is by car. There are many car hire companies in the Azores including **Ilha Verde** and **Autatlantis**, which have offices at airports and various towns across the archipelago. To hire a car you will need to produce a valid driving licence and a passport or other form of official identification. Rates tend to be cheaper in the low season. An alternative to hiring a car is to rent a scooter, which still requires all the necessary documentation, but is a far cheaper method of transport.

DIRECTORY

ARRIVING BY AIR

Aeroportas de Portugal
w ana.pt

Azores Express
c (508) 677 0555 (US)

easyJet
w easyjet.com

Horta Airport, Faial
c (292) 943 511
w aeroportohorta.pt

João Paulo II Airport, São Miguel
c (296) 205 400
w aeroportoponta
delgada.pt

Lajes Airport, Terceira
c (295) 540 047
w aerogarelajes.azores.
gov.pt

Ryanair
c (0871) 246 0000 (UK)
w ryanair.com

SATA
c (707) 227 282
w sata.pt

SATA Express
c (416) 515 7188
(Canada)

TAP Air Portugal
c (707) 205 700
w flytap.com

ARRIVING BY SEA

Azores Marinas
w marinasazores.com

Portas do Mar
c (296) 281 500
w portasdomar.pt

Porto da Horta
c (292) 293 453
w portosdosacores.pt

Praia da Vitória
c (295) 540 000

ISLAND-HOPPING BY SEA

Atlanticoline
c (707) 201 572
w atlanticoline.pt

Triangle The Azores
c (292) 679 505
w triangletheazores.com

TRAVELLING BY BUS

S. Miguel Transportes
w smigueltransportes.
com

Transportes Açores
w azoresapi.com

UTC
w utcazores.com

TRAVELLING BY TAXI

Azorean Tours
w azoreantours.com

TRAVELLING BY CAR

Autatlantis
c (296) 205 340
w autatlantis.com

Ilha Verde
c (296) 304 891
w ilhaverde.com

Practical Information

Passports and Visas

Visitors from outside the European Economic Area (EEA), European Union (EU) and Switzerland need a valid passport to enter Portugal. EEA, EU and Swiss nationals can use their identity cards instead. Those arriving from New Zealand, USA, Australia and Canada can stay for a maximum of 90 days in any half-year without a visa. Citizens from other countries need a visa and should check ahead at the Portuguese embassy or consulate in their own country. Schengen visas are valid. The website of the **Secretary of State for Portuguese Communities** states visa requirements.

Embassies and Consulates

Embassies and consulates located in Ponta Delgada and Lisbon, including those of the **UK**, **USA**, **Canada** and **Australia**, provide services for nationals visiting the Azores.

Customs Regulations

It is illegal to export scrimshaw and other items made from whale teeth and bone. There are no limits on the amount of alcohol and tobacco visitors can bring in from EU countries, but larger quantities can be seized if customs feel they are of a commercial nature. The **Visa HQ** website outlines import/export limitations for those travelling from outside the EU.

Travel Safety Advice

Visitors can get up-to-date travel safety information from the **UK Foreign and Commonwealth Office**, the **US Department of State** and the **Australian Department of Foreign Affairs and Trade**.

Travel Insurance

Comprehensive travel insurance is recommended for visitors. Adventure tourists can purchase additional cover for high-risk activities such as watersports, horse riding and canyoning.

All EU nationals visiting the Azores are entitled to arrangements covering medical care and expenses, except dental care. British nationals should carry their European Health Insurance Card (EHIC), which covers "necessary medical treatment" only.

Health

Vaccinations are not required for foreign visitors to the Azores, though anyone arriving from a country where yellow fever is prevalent will need to show proof of inoculation. The three main hospitals in the Azores are **Divino Espírito Santo**, São Miguel, **Hospital da Horta**, Faial and **Hospital de Santo Espírito**, Terceira. The former two are equipped with hyperbaric chambers.

Healthcare facilities are basic outside the main towns. Walk-in health centres, known as *centros de saúde*, provide check-ups and non-emergency treatment. The **Centro de Saúde de Santa Cruz das Flores** has a hyperbaric chamber. *Farmácias* (pharmacies) are widespread and identified by their green cross signage. Tap water is safe to drink; however, water sourced from fountains should be avoided, particularly those noted as *água não potável* (not suitable for drinking).

Emergency Services

The police, ambulance and fire brigade can be reached on the nationwide emergency number 112. The operators speak English and calls are free.

Personal Security

The Azores are considered a safe destination for visitors, including solo female travellers, but it is still wise to take precautions against theft, such as never leaving valuables unattended. Theft should be reported to the authorities as soon as possible. You will need an official police report signed to present to your insurers in order to make a claim. There is a 24-hour **Tourist Police** division in Ponta Delgada. Theft or loss of documents, such as your passport, should be reported to your consulate.

Currency and Banking

Portugal's unit of currency is the euro. Banknotes of denominations greater than €50 are not widely circulated or readily accepted as payment.

Some establishments prefer to work with smaller denominations. Currency exchange is available at **Nova Câmbios** in Ponta Delgada airport and most banks: look for the desks marked *câmbios*. Banking hours are 8:30am to 3pm Monday to Friday. The most convenient way of getting funds is via an ATM, known as *multibanco* or MB. These are located in and outside most banks, public transport hubs and shopping centres. Traveller's cheques are not widely accepted and are best avoided.

Without a credit card, you will not be able to rent a car or check into a hotel. Visa and MasterCard are accepted everywhere; American Express and Diners Club cards less so.

Telephone and Internet

The country code for Portugal is 00351. The islands also have codes: 296 for São Miguel and Santa Maria; 295 for Terceira, Graciosa and São Jorge; 292 for Pico, Faial, Flores and Corvo. Most public telephone booths only accept a *cartão telefónico* (telephone chargecard), available from post offices, kiosks and newsagents.

Many of the islands' hotels and guesthouses offer complimentary Wi-Fi. Free Internet access is also available at Ponta Delgada, Lajes and Horta airports and in lots of bars, cafés, restaurants and larger shopping malls.

To use your mobile phone in the Azores, it will need to be equipped for GSM network frequencies 900 and 1800 MHz. To avoid running up high roaming fees purchase a local SIM card and take advantage of local rates. Check with your home carrier if you need to unlock your device to use a different SIM card/service.

Postal Services

The Portuguese postal service is known as the **CTT Correios de Portugal**. *Correios* (post offices) are usually open from 9am to 6pm on weekdays. First-class mail, known as *correio azul*, is posted in blue postboxes, everything else in red postboxes.

DIRECTORY

PASSPORTS AND VISAS

Secretary of State for Portuguese Communities
w secomunidades.pt/vistos

EMBASSIES AND CONSULATES

Australian Embassy
Avenida da Liberdade 200, 2nd Floor, Lisbon, Portugal
((213) 101 500

British Consulate General
Rua de São Bernardo 33, Lisbon, Portugal
((213) 924 000

Canadian Embassy
Avenida da Liberdade 198–200, 3rd Floor, Lisbon, Portugal
((213) 164 600

United States Consulate General
MAP U1 ■ Avenida Príncipe do Mónaco 6, Ponta Delgada, São Miguel
((296) 308 330

CUSTOMS REGULATIONS

Visa HQ
w portugal.visahq.com/customs

TRAVEL SAFETY ADVICE

Australian Department of Foreign Affairs and Trade
w dfat.gov.au
w smartraveller.gov.au

UK Foreign and Commonwealth Office
w gov.uk/foreign-travel-advice

US Department of State
w travel.state.gov

HEALTH

Centro de Saúde de Santa Cruz das Flores
MAP R5 ■ Largo 25 de Abril, Santa Cruz das Flores, Flores
((292) 590 270

Divino Espírito Santo Hospital
MAP B6 ■ Avenida D Manuel I, Ponta Delgada, São Miguel
((296) 203 000

Hospital da Horta
MAP S3 ■ Estrada Príncipe Alberto do Mónaco, Horta, Faial
((292) 201 000

Hospital de Santo Espírito
MAP M6 ■ Canada do Briado, Angra do Heroísmo, Terceira
((295) 403 200

PERSONAL SECURITY

Tourist Police
MAP V2 ■ Polícia de Segurança Pública, Rua da Alfândega, Ponta Delgada, São Miguel
((296) 282 022

CURRENCY AND BANKING

Nova Câmbios
MAP B6 ■ João Paulo II Airport, Ponta Delgada, São Miguel
Open 7am–4pm daily
((296) 306 770

POSTAL SERVICES

CTT Correios de Portugal
w ctt.pt

Newspapers, Magazines, TV and Radio

Founded in 1835, *Açoreano Oriental* is Portugal's oldest newspaper. Together with *Diário Insular*, these are the main Portuguese newspapers. Also published in Portuguese is the online magazine *Azores Today*, which has a festivals and events calendar. *RTP Açores* provides local radio and TV news services.

Opening Hours

Shops are generally open from 9am to 1pm and 2 to 6pm from Monday to Friday and 9am to 1:30pm on Saturday. In the towns, business hours at larger stores often carry through the lunch hour. Shopping malls such as Parque Atlântico remain open from 9am to 11pm daily. In rural areas, shops are likely to be closed on weekends.

Time Difference

The islands are 1 hour behind Greenwich Mean Time (GMT) and 4 hours ahead of US Eastern Standard Time (EST). The clock moves forward 1 hour during daylight saving time, from the last Sunday in March to the last Sunday in October.

Electrical Appliances

The islands use plugs with two round pins and a voltage of 220V. Most hotels offer built-in adaptors for electric razors.

Weather

An all-year destination, the Azores enjoy a mild temperate climate, with the average temperature varying between 11° C and 26° C (51° F and 78° F). June, July and August are the warmest months. April, May, September and October have pleasant weather. November to March can see wet, windy days with sporadic sunshine. However, the Azores are prone to rainfall at any time of the year.

The high season runs from mid-June to mid-September. Summer also sees more restaurants and bars open and a full cultural calendar of island-wide festivals and events.

Travellers with Special Needs

The Azores are slowly addressing the requirements of travellers with mobility issues. SATA *(see p107)* offers ground and in-flight assistance to passengers with special physical needs or disabilities. Similarly, TAP Air Portugal *(see p107)* offers support through the MyWay service. **Accessible Portugal** can arrange hotel and airport transfers using vehicles adapted for wheelchairs. **Disabled Holidays** lists hotels suitable for guests with limited mobility and can arrange travel insurance which caters for disabilities and pre-existing medical conditions. **Cresaçor** *(see p15)* is a pioneer of inclusive tourism in the archipelago and is listed on the **European Network for Accessible Tourism**. Some hotels are adapting their facilities to meet the demands of wheelchair-bound guests, as are selected museums, some of which also provide information in Braille.

Sources of Information

The **Visit Azores** website provides a list of tourist offices, approved accommodation, and sightseeing and practical information. **Art Azores** lists walking routes and places to eat, while **Parques Naturais** describes the islands' natural parks. The **Tourist Helpline** provides a good overview of the region. **Spot Azores** offers information about weather conditions. The app **Whimzr Azores** allows access to a range of restaurant, shopping and other activities. Similarly, the **Percursos do Artesanato dos Açores** app provides lists of handicraft workshops and places to shop for arts and crafts. *Triângulo Magazine* is aimed at travellers visiting São Jorge, Pico and Faial. The blogs posted on **Epicure and Culture** showcase Azorean handicraft culture and artisanal cuisine.

Trips and Tours

Well-established UK tour operators offering trips to the Azores include **Archipelago Choice** and **Sunvil**. **Biosphere Expeditions** and **Nature Trek** lean towards a more scientific and conservational experience while **Portugal Walks** organizes self-guided walks. US-based **Tour Azores** provides escorted tours. **Sunmed Holidays** in Canada include the Azores in their programmes.

Melo Agência de Viagens in Ponta Delgada offers walking holidays. **Turis Verde** specializes in nature and environmental tourism.

Shopping

Buying items such as woven bedspreads and embroidered tablecloths helps sustain a centuries-old tradition. Purchasing cheese from São Jorge, wine from Pico, pekoe from Europe's only tea plantation (see p68), or jewellery made from basalt will speak of your travels. **Made in Azores**, an online shopping site, features traditional goods. Non-EU residents shopping in the Azores can claim back VAT on purchases over €61.35. The **Global Blue** website has more details.

Dining

The greatest variety of restaurants are in and around Ponta Delgada, Angra do Heroísmo and Horta. Dishes such as *alcatra* and *polvo guisado* (octopus in red wine sauce) can be found here. In recent years internationally trained chefs have been creating imaginatively presented fusion cuisine. Local fish and seafood is a speciality, and the best restaurants for an ocean harvest are located on the water's edge. All eateries are non-smoking, although tables set on outside terraces are exempt from this rule. Tipping is not customary, but if you feel the food and service is exceptional, 10 per cent of the total amount is more than enough.

Where to Stay

There are two five-star hotels in São Miguel and one in Terceira. Many historic hotels – converted forts, manor houses and convent buildings – offer upscale accommodation. The majority fall within the mid-range, four-star category. Numerous B&Bs and traditionally styled guesthouses are listed on the **Casas Açorianas** website. The budget traveller can opt for a *pensão* or *residencial* – clean, basic accommodation. Another idea is to check into a hostel or book on **Airbnb.** There are five youth hostels operated by **Azores Pousadas de Juventude**. All islands have official campsites; the Visit Azores website lists most.

DIRECTORY

NEWSPAPERS, MAGAZINES, TV AND RADIO

Açoreano Oriental
w acorianooriental.pt

Azores Today
w azorestoday.com

Diário Insular
w diarioinsular.pt

RTP Açores
w rtp.pt/acores

TRAVELLERS WITH SPECIAL NEEDS

Accessible Portugal
w accessibleportugal.com

Cresaçor
w azoresforall.com

Disabled Holidays
w disabledholidays.com

European Network for Accessible Tourism
w accessibletourism.org

SOURCES OF INFORMATION

Art Azores
w en.artazores.com

Epicure and Culture
w epicureandculture.com

Parques Naturais
w parquesnaturais.azores. gov.pt

Percursos do Artesanato dos Açores
w artesanato.azores.gov.pt

Spot Azores
w spotazores.com

Tourist Helpline
((296) 284 569

Triângulo Magazine
w triangulomagazine.com

Visit Azores
w visitazores.com

Whimzr Azores
w whimzr.com

TRIPS AND TOURS

Archipelago Choice
w archipelagochoice.com

Biosphere Expeditions
w biosphere-expeditions. org

Melo Agência de Viagens
w melotravel.com

Nature Trek
w naturetrek.co.uk

Portugal Walks
w portugalwalks.com

Sunmed Holidays
w sunmedholidays.com

Sunvil
w sunvil.co.uk

Tour Azores
w tourazores.com

Turis Verde
w turisverde.com

SHOPPING

Global Blue
w globalblue.com

Made in Azores
w madeinazores.eu

WHERE TO STAY

Airbnb
w airbnb.com

Azores Pousadas de Juventude
w pousadasjuvacores.com

Casas Açorianas
w casasacorianas.com

Places to Stay

Historic Hotels

Casa do Campo de São Francisco

MAP U2 ▪ Campo de São Francisco 15–17, Ponta Delgada, São Miguel ▪ (296) 287 144 ▪ casacampo saofrancisco.com ▪ €€
Antique furnishings add to the authenticity of this impressive 18th-century mansion. The building features three rooms and two suites decorated to reflect the Baroque period. Breakfast is a feast of Azorean produce laid out on tiled tabletops.

Casa da Torre

MAP N3 ▪ Estrada Regional 37, Companhia de Baixo São João, Lajes do Pico, Pico ▪ (962) 432 694 ▪ www.picotheazores. com/casadatorre ▪ €€
Built in 1916, this quirky accommodation option stands out for its unusual architecture and the small tower that still retains a traditional wind turbine once used to generate power for light bulbs.

Convento de São Francisco

MAP D6 ▪ Jardim António Silva Cabral, Vila Franca do Campo, São Miguel ▪ (296) 583 532 ▪ convento saofrancisco.net ▪ €€
A perfect place for those seeking peace and solitude, this former 16th-century convent has been renovated as an elegant retreat. Each room is decorated with contemporary and religious art, exotic wood and rich fabrics.

Hotel do Colégio

MAP U2 ▪ Rua Carvalho Araújo 39, Ponta Delgada, São Miguel ▪ (296) 306 600 ▪ hotel docolegio.com ▪ €€
The beautiful vaulted ceilings that grace the lounge and bar add historic character to this attractive hotel. The building dates from the 19th century and was previously a music conservatory.

Pousada Forte Angra do Heroísmo

MAP M6 ▪ Rua do Castelinho, Angra do Heroísmo, Terceira ▪ (295) 403 560 ▪ DA ▪ www. pousadas.pt ▪ €€
Located behind the historic 16th-century walls of the former Castelo de São Sebastião on a dramatic coastline are 28 modern rooms and one suite of exceptional character. The most atmospheric are those housed in the refurbished governor's house.

Quinta do Espírito Santo

MAP M6 ▪ Rua Dr Teotónio Machado Pires 36, Angra do Heroísmo, Terceira ▪ (295) 332 373 ▪ www. quintadoespiritosanto. com ▪ €€
Owner Francisco Maduro-Dias is the former director for the office of restoration of Angra do Heroísmo's World Heritage Site. Together with his wife, he welcomes guests to their gorgeous home, an 18th-century landmark.

Quinta de Nossa Senhora das Mercês

MAP M6 ▪ Caminho de Baixo, São Mateus, Angra do Heroísmo, Terceira ▪ (295) 642 588 ▪ quinta dasmerces.com ▪ €€
This grand country manor was built in the 17th century. In keeping with its historical patrimony, the hotel features classically styled rooms. The highlight is the infinity pool with its Atlantic panorama.

Solar de Lalém

MAP D5 ▪ Estrada de São Pedro, Maia, São Miguel ▪ (296) 442 004 ▪ www. solardelalem.com ▪ €€
A beautifully preserved 1687-built chapel dedicated to São Sebastião is the oldest part of this property. Once the residence of 17th-century aristocrats, the manor house features individually decorated rooms with antique furnishings.

Pousada Forte da Horta

MAP T3 ▪ Rua Vasco da Gama, Horta, Faial ▪ (292) 202 200 ▪ DA ▪ www.pousadas.pt ▪ €€€
Once impregnable, the 16th-century Forte de Santa Cruz is today a charming hotel overlooking Horta's harbour and the colourful marina. The Sal & Pico Restaurant serves regional cuisine with wines from Portugal.

Terra Nostra Garden Hotel

MAP E5 ▪ Rua Padre José Jacinto Botelho 5, Furnas, São Miguel ▪ (296) 549 090 ▪ www.bensaude.pt ▪ €€€

Dating back to the 1930s, this is one of the most emblematic hotels in the Azores. The original building still retains Art Deco flourishes. Residents enjoy free access to the famous 18th-century park.

Eco and Nature Hotels

7 Cidades Lake Lodge

MAP A5 ▪ Rua das Lavadeiras 2, Sete Cidades, São Miguel ▪ (918) 304 014 ▪ 7cidadeslakelodge. com ▪ €€

Stay in lakefront bungalows set on the tranquil shores of Lagoa Azul. The wood-wrapped accommodation blends perfectly with the environment and provides all modern conveniences.

Aldeia da Cuada

MAP R6 ▪ Aldeia da Cuada, Lajes do Flores, Flores ▪ (292) 590 040 ▪ aldeiadacuada.com ▪ €€

This once-abandoned village of 14 stone cottages is now one of the Azores' most celebrated rural resorts. The buildings have been refurbished as fully equipped one-, two- and six-bedroomed units.

Aldeia da Fonte

MAP N3 ▪ Caminho de Baixo, Silveira, Lajes do Pico, Pico ▪ (292) 679 500 ▪ www.aldeiada fonte.com ▪ €€

These volcanic stone cottages house studios and suites. The cliffside estate is visited by a great variety of birds. Nights see the arrival of Azores noctule bats, the archipelago's only endemic mammal.

Jardim do Triângulo

MAP N1 ▪ Eco Triângulo, Terreiros 91, Velas, São Jorge ▪ (295) 414 055 ▪ www.ecotriangulo. com ▪ €€

A complimentary bottle of wine is offered to guests along with the keys to their basalt stone cottages, set over a landscaped garden in the grounds of an 18th-century country house. On clear days Pico island looks close enough to touch.

Quinta das Buganvílias

MAP H3 ▪ Quinta das Buganvílias 28A, Faial ▪ (292) 943 255 ▪ quinta dasbuganvilias.com ▪ €€

Accommodation here is on a well-maintained organic farm. Rooms are available in the main building and the stone annexe. The grounds feature camellias, bougainvillea, orchids and magnolias, along with guava and banana trees.

Quinta do Martelo

MAP M6 ▪ Canada do Martelo 24, São Francisco das Almas, São Mateus, Terceira ▪ (962) 812 796 ▪ quintadomartelo.net ▪ €€

Experience an authentic countryside stay at this charming homestead. Four types of accommodation options are available, including the cosy stone-clad "settler's houses".

Quinta da Meia Eira

MAP H3 ▪ Rua dos Inocentes 1, Castelo Branco, Horta, Faial ▪ (292) 943 037 ▪ www.meiaeira.com ▪ €€

Bright and colourful, this imaginatively renovated farmhouse is family run and features cottages and rooms that are traditionally furnished and surrounded by gardens flecked with flowers. The solarium is a winter bonus.

Quinta da Terça

MAP C6 ▪ Rua Padre Domingos 221, Livramento, São Miguel ▪ (296) 642 134 ▪ www.quintadaterca.com ▪ €€

An equestrian theme runs through this farmhouse, which is part of a working stable. It is geared towards riders seeking a base from which to explore the island. Guest rooms are individually furnished and a stay includes breakfast.

Pestana Bahia Praia – Nature & Beach Resort

MAP D6 ▪ Praia de Água d'Alto, Vila Franca do Campo, São Miguel ▪ (296) 539 130 ▪ www.pestana.com ▪ €€€

During summer, guests are regaled by the strange nasal cries of Cory's shearwaters nesting on nearby cliffs, a sea life soundtrack that adds appeal to this secluded resort. Oceanside views embrace a wide, sandy bay.

Santa Bárbara Eco-Beach Resort

MAP C5 ▪ Estrada Regional 1, Morro de Baixo-Ribeira Seca, Ribeira Grande, São Miguel ▪ (296) 470 360 ▪ santabarbaraazores. com ▪ €€€

Located along an idyllic coastline, this villa complex features minimalist architectural design and has an appealing, organic quality. A restaurant, bar and beach club offer pleasant distractions.

Contemporary Hotels

Graciosa Resort & Business Hotel

MAP K5 ▪ Porto da Barra, Santa Cruz da Graciosa, Graciosa ▪ (295) 730 500 ▪ €€

Flanked by vineyards and with views over the scenic bay of Cais da Barra, accommodation here is divided between rooms, suites and villas. Leisure facilities extend to a pool and sauna, while the Aroma Restaurant adds a dash of sophistication.

Hotel do Canal

MAP T3 ▪ Largo Dr Manuel de Arriaga, Horta, Faial ▪ (292) 202 120 ▪ www.bensaude.pt ▪ €€

Rooms facing the harbour offer inspiring views of the marina and nearby Pico – a breathtaking panorama at any time of the day. Located in the town centre, the hotel's amenities include a fitness centre, a sauna and the Clipper Restaurant.

Hotel Colombo

MAP E2 ▪ Rua Cruz Teixeira, Vila do Porto, Santa Maria ▪ (296) 820 200 ▪ www.colombo-hotel.com ▪ €€

Hugely popular in the summer months, this hotel has plenty of amenities to keep guests occupied, including a pool, Jacuzzi and Turkish bath. There is also a play park for kids.

Hotel das Flores

MAP R5 ▪ Zona do Boqueirão, Santa Cruz das Flores, Flores ▪ (292) 590 420 ▪ www.inatel.pt ▪ €€

All 26 rooms at this smart hotel near the whaling museum have superb views of distant Corvo. The interior is decorated with black-and-white images of whales, sharks and other marine life. A well-stocked bar, excellent restaurant and outside pool complete the picture.

Hotel Terceira Mar

MAP M6 ▪ Portões de São Pedro, Angra do Heroísmo, Terceira ▪ (295) 402 280 ▪ DA ▪ www.bensaude.pt ▪ €€

Not far from the UNESCO-listed historic centre, this handsome property overlooks a bay. A health club, an outdoor seawater pool and the Monte Brasil Restaurant encourage rest and relaxation. The hotel is noted for its environmental management.

Hotel Vila Nova

MAP U2 ▪ Rua João Francisco Cabral 1/3, Ponta Delgada, São Miguel ▪ (296) 301 600 ▪ www.vilanovahotel.com ▪ €€

Comfortable and functional, this modern hotel is ideal for families and business travellers seeking a base near the historic centre. A breakfast and dinner buffet is offered. Guests can take advantage of an outdoor pool.

Royal Garden Hotel

MAP U2 ▪ Rua de Lisboa, Ponta Delgada, São Miguel ▪ (296) 307 300 ▪ www.azoreshotelroyalgarden.com ▪ €€

Accommodation at this upscale hotel includes spacious, well-appointed family rooms. It is also possible to place an extra cot or assemble a daybed in the senior suite. Business travellers will appreciate the meetings and events facilities.

Azor

MAP V2 ▪ Avenida Dr João Bosco Mota Amaral, São Miguel ▪ (296) 249 900 ▪ www.azorhotel.com ▪ €€€

Stay at this hotel for its cutting-edge interior design and wonderful views from the rooms. The Azor raises the bar with first-rate amenities, such as the daringly stylish rooftop pool. Downstairs, the Lobby Market combines a fabulous restaurant with an innovative Wine & Cheese Corner.

Caloura Hotel Resort

MAP C6 ▪ Rua do Jublieu 27, Água de Pau, São Miguel ▪ (296) 960 900 ▪ calourahotel.com ▪ €€€

This resort is set over a secluded bay with direct access both to the sea and a cluster of natural pools surrounded by volcanic rock. There is also a freshwater pool. Rooms and suites have splendid ocean views, and the in-house Barrocas do Mar Restaurant offers a wide choice of meat and seasonal fish dishes.

Pedras do Mar Resort & Spa

MAP B5 ▪ Rua das Terças 3, Fenais da Luz, São Miguel ▪ (296) 249 300 ▪ www.pedrasdomar.com ▪ €€€

An airport shuttle service whisks guests off to this peaceful resort, located on the water's edge. Family-orientated, the place has a relaxing vibe that is accentuated by its sports amenities and a modest spa facility. The out-of-the-way location, however, means you will need a vehicle to explore further.

B&Bs

Guest House Comodoro

MAP R4 ▪ Caminho do Areeiro, Vila do Corvo, Corvo ▪ (292) 596 128 ▪ www.comodoro azores.com ▪ €

Family-managed and renowned for its hospitality, this is still the only decent accommodation option on tiny Corvo. The guesthouse has 14 rooms, five with wooden deck terraces. Guests can request a free transfer from the airport. Book ahead for summer and autumn stays.

Casa do António

MAP N1 ▪ Rua Infante D. Henrique 21, Velas, São Jorge ▪ (295) 430 330 ▪ Closed Nov–Mar ▪ www. casadoantonio.com ▪ €€

Every floor of this B&B affords a wonderful view, but the rooms facing Pico island paint a picture of serenity. Its blue-and-white façade is easily discernible from the harbour. The buffet-style breakfast served here is one of the most popular on the island.

Casa das Faias

MAP K5 ▪ Rua Infante D. Henrique 9, Praia, Graciosa ▪ (295) 732 766 ▪ www.casas acorianas.com ▪ €€

Wrapped in patterned basalt stonework, the rustic tone of this rambling inn is deliberate, despite being located just a short distance out of town. The lounge on the top floor affords a lovely panoramic view of the bay. Breakfast is sometimes an ad-hoc affair, where you make your own from a freshly stocked fridge.

Pensão Francisca

MAP E2 ▪ Brejo de Baixo, Almagreira, Santa Maria ▪ (296) 884 033 ▪ www. azorean-spirit.com ▪ €€

Spotless rooms and a separate cottage are on offer here, all within walking distance of the Praia Formosa beach (see pp68–9). The friendly hosts can arrange outdoor activities, including yoga.

Quinta do Canavial

MAP M1 ▪ Quinta do Canavial, Velas, São Jorge ▪ (918) 904 568 ▪ www. aquintadocanavial.com ▪ €€

The owners of this traditional guesthouse are keen hikers and have compiled a local walking guide for their guests. The breakfast patio peers over a secluded bay and there is a seasonal pool sunk into the terrace.

Residencia Argonauta

MAP Q6 ▪ Rua Senador André de Freitas 5, Fajã Grande, Flores ▪ (292) 552 219 ▪ Closed 1 Nov–19 Dec ▪ www.argonauta-flores.com ▪ €€

Decorated with prints, photographs and various collectibles, rooms in this quirky house are adorned with volcanic rock and wood, some of it originating from a shipwreck. Dating from 1929, the building still features the first bathroom built in the village.

Solar da Glória ao Carmo

MAP C6 ▪ Rua da Glória ao Carmo 5, Livramento, Ponta Delgada, São Miguel ▪ (296) 629 847 ▪ www. gloriaaocarmo.com ▪ €€

One double room, two spacious suites and a pair of custom-built apartments

provide accommodation at this handsome 18th-century country manor. The breakfast changes daily and can be taken at any hour of the day.

Vila Bélgica

MAP J3 ▪ Caminho Velho da Caldeira 13, Horta, Faial ▪ (292) 392 614 ▪ www. azoresvilabelgica.com ▪ €€

On a clear day, views of neighbouring Pico island from this cosy B&B are memorable. So, too, is the combination of "Stay and Sail", where guests staying during the summer can combine a few days at the guesthouse with a private mini-cruise aboard the schooner Elise Picard.

Vivenda da Saudade

MAP M6 ▪ Estrada Regional 14, São Mateus da Calheta, Angra do Heroísmo, Terceira ▪ (295) 643 105 ▪ www.vivenda dasaudade.com ▪ Open Jun–Sep ▪ €€

A rural location with sea views is reason enough to stay at this immaculately maintained B&B. The fact that it is a 10-minute drive from Angra do Heroísmo is a plus, but the amiable hosts, Al and Vilma, are the deal clincher.

Whale'come Residencial

MAP N3 ▪ Rua dos Baleeiros, Lajes do Pico, Pico ▪ (292) 672 010 ▪ hotel.espacotalassa. com ▪ €€

Anchored to the Espaço Talassa whale-watching operation (see p17), this maritime-themed residencial features bright breezy rooms with modern amenities. It is incredibly popular, so you need to book early, even in winter.

For a key to hotel price categories see p112

Boutique Hotels

Hotel Charming Blue

MAP E2 ▪ Rua Teófilo de Braga 31, Vila do Porto, Santa Maria ▪ (296) 882 107 ▪ www.charming blue.com ▪ €€

The classical veneer belies the modernity of this lovely townhouse. Rooms are contemporary and elegantly designed, and the restaurant sets new culinary standards. Other amenities include a modest spa.

Hotel Praia Marina

MAP P5 ▪ Avenida Beira Mar, Praia da Vitória, Terceira ▪ (295) 540 055 ▪ www.hotelpraiamarina. com ▪ €€

Bright, modern studio apartments offer splendid balcony views over the beach and the nearby marina. Functional and reliable, the hotel is just a short walk from the town centre.

Hotel Talisman

MAP U2 ▪ Rua Marquês da Praia e Monforte 40, Ponta Delgada, São Miguel ▪ (296) 308 500 ▪ www. hoteltalisman.com ▪ €€

Centrally located, the building dates back to the 17th century and retains its period charm, exemplified by the romantic Palm Terrace Restaurant. The guest experience here is heightened by a sun-trapping rooftop pool.

Pico do Refúgio

MAP C5 ▪ Roda do Pico 5, Rabo de Peixe, Ribeira Grande, São Miguel ▪ (296) 491 062 ▪ DA ▪ www.picodorefugio. com ▪ €€

A 17th-century country manor house has been carefully refurbished into superbly appointed apartments and lofts. Guests can walk the farmland (an ecological reserve) and there is even an on-site diving school. Ideal for couples and families.

Baía da Barca

MAP L2 ▪ Lugar da Barca, Madalena, Pico ▪ (292) 628 750 ▪ DA ▪ www. baiadabarca.com ▪ €€€

Seemingly chiselled out of basalt, these comfortable and convenient eco-friendly apartments are set on the water's edge. Guests can take advantage of a saltwater pool, and the Atlantic Ocean and Pico mountain views never cease to please.

Casa Hintze Ribeiro

MAP U2 ▪ Rua Hintze Ribeiro 62, Ponta Delgada, São Miguel ▪ (296) 304 340 ▪ www.casahintze ribeiro.com ▪ €€€

Named after the famous Portuguese politician Ernesto Hintze Ribeiro (1849–1907), this smart, design-led hotel bears the hallmarks of interior designer Nini Andrade Silva. The one-bedroom apartments feature kitchenettes and some have city-view terraces.

Furnas Boutique Hotel

MAP E5 ▪ Avenida Dr Manuel de Arriaga, Furnas, São Miguel ▪ (296) 249 200 ▪ www.furnasboutique hotel.com ▪ €€€

Earthy tones, lots of dark wood and communal areas embellished with plants – this Zen-like retreat is designed around an attractive spa that offers a thermal pool, massage, reflexology and a range of treatments and therapies. The À Terra restaurant is noted for its healthy menu.

Furnas Lake Villas

MAP E6 ▪ Estrada Regional do Sul, Lagoa das Furnas, Furnas, São Miguel ▪ (296) 584 107 ▪ www.furnaslakevillas.pt ▪ €€€

These villas follow a minimalist Scandinavian style, inspired by local rustic granaries. The hotel is ideally placed for exploring the surrounding area, although a vehicle is recommended. Guests can sign up for outdoor activities. Breakfast can be served in the apartments.

Pocinho Bay

MAP L2 ▪ Pocinho, Candelária, Pico ▪ (292) 629 135 ▪ www.pocinho bay.com ▪ €€€

Located near Pico's UNESCO-listed vineyards (see pp32–3), this charming retreat melds innovative interior design with a traditional home-style ambience. Each room is individually styled, and the views across the channel to Faial are beautiful.

Quinta do Mar

MAP C6 ▪ Rua da Portela 43, Caloura, Água de Pau, São Miguel ▪ (296) 913 990 ▪ quintadomar-caloura.com ▪ €€€

This contemporary and stylish bolthole has been imaginatively fashioned out of a former winery. Amid tranquil gardens overlooking the sea, the en-suite rooms are set around an inviting open-air swimming pool. Breakfast and snacks are served in the airy garden pavilion.

Budget Hotels

A Casa do Lado
MAP T2 ■ Rua D. Pedro IV 23, Horta, Faial ■ (292) 700 351 ■ www.acasa dolado.com ■ €

Dario and Vanessa, the young couple who run this traditionally styled guesthouse, are passionate about the environment and share with guests their enthusiasm for lowering the hotel's carbon footprint. Rooms are simply furnished and have private bathrooms.

Guest House Malheiros Serpa
MAP R5 ■ Casa de Hóspedes, Malheiros Serpa, Rua do Hospital 8, Santa Cruz das Flores, Flores ■ (292) 592 201 ■ www.malheiros.net ■ €

Doubles and singles are available at this centrally located homely guesthouse, with all rooms featuring en-suite bathrooms. Guests have full use of amenities, including a fully equipped kitchen. There is also a self-contained cottage available for rent on a monthly or yearly basis.

Hotel Carvalho Araújo
MAP U2 ■ Rua Carvalho Araújo 63–65, Ponta Delgada, São Miguel ■ (296) 307 090 ■ DA ■ www.azoreshotelca. com ■ €

A basic option located on a quiet backstreet, Caravalho Araújo offers comfortable rooms with private bathrooms and cable TVs. Public areas include a lounge, mini bar and a dining room. A laundry service is available on request.

In53 Guest House
MAP U2 ■ Rua João Francisco Cabral 53, Ponta Delgada, São Miguel ■ (296) 642 549 ■ in53 guesthouse.com ■ €

Pinewood flooring, patterned fabrics and an elegant, home-style ambience characterize this guesthouse. Three rooms, one of them furnished with bunk beds, allow for various guest configurations. The kitchen, bathrooms and lounge are communal. The double room require a minimum two-night stay.

The Nook
MAP U1 ■ Travessa do Pedro Homem 2, Ponta Delgada, São Miguel ■ (296) 703 159 ■ www. thenookhostel.com ■ €

A brilliant example of how the Azores' burgeoning hostel sector is appealing to budget travellers with hotel-grade properties, this contemporary place close to the town centre offers a choice between shared and private rooms. Some of the rooms require a minimum two-night stay. There is a fully equipped kitchen, laundry service and lockers.

Residencial Bela Vista
MAP N3 ■ Avenida Marginal 1, Lajes do Pico, Pico ■ (962) 413 409 ■ DA ■ www. lajesbelavista.com ■ €

Doubles, singles, triples and studios are quickly snapped up here over the summer. The lovely one-bedroom self-catering apartment is a delight to stay in. This is an ideal location for joining a whale-watching excursion or for exploring the island's eastern tip.

Residencial Branco
MAP P5 ■ Estrada 25 de Abril 2, Praia da Vitória, Terceira ■ (295) 513 459 ■ DA ■ www.residencial-branco.com ■ €

This spruce guesthouse sits in a quiet corner of the town, but is within walking distance of the beach. All rooms have cable TVs and private bathrooms.

Residencial Neto
MAP N1 ■ Rua Conselheiro Dr José Pereira 12, Velas, São Jorge ■ (295) 432 106 ■ €

The first accommodation option at which you arrive after stepping off the ferry, this no-frills choice exudes a faded charm. They can arrange airport shuttles and bicycle hire. The rooftop pool is lovely.

Residencial Santa Cruz
MAP J5 ■ Largo Barão de Guadalupe 9, Santa Cruz da Graciosa, Graciosa ■ (295) 712 345 ■ residencial santacruz.pt ■ €

Located on a terrace of traditional whitewashed townhouses, this guesthouse has 18 rooms with bathrooms and TVs. It is only 100 m (109 yards) from the sea, and a short walk from town.

Residencial São Miguel
MAP U2 ■ Rua Dr Bruno Tavares Carreiro 28, Ponta Delgada, São Miguel ■ (296) 286 086 ■ www. residencialsaomiguel. com ■ €

There are 20 rooms with private bathrooms and cable TVs at this pleasant guesthouse situated in the historic downtown area. A continental breakfast is included in the rate.

For a key to hotel price categories see p112

Index

Acknowledgments

Author

Paul Bernhardt is a British freelance travel writer and photographer based in Portugal. He has authored *DK Eyewitness Top 10 Travel Guide: Algarve*, and has provided editorial and revision assistance for *DK Eyewitness Travel Guide: Portugal* and *DK Eyewitness Top 10 Travel Guide: Madeira*. For this title he would like to thank his editors and the team at Azores Promotion Board for their help and encouragement.

Publishing Director Georgina Dee

Publisher Vivien Antwi

Design Director Phil Ormerod

Editorial Ankita Awasthi Tröger, Michelle Crane, Shikha Kulkarni, Maresa Manara, Akshay Rana, Sally Schafer, Avijit Sengupta

Design Tessa Bindloss, Richard Czapnik, Priyanka Thakur, Vinita Venugopal

Picture Research Susie Peachey, Ellen Root, Lucy Sienkowska, Oran Tarjan

Cartography Mohammad Hassan, Suresh Kumar, Casper Morris
Maps in this book are derived from © OpenStreetMap contributors, see www.openstreetmap.org/copyright for further details.

DTP Jason Little, Azeem Siddiqui, Tanveer Abbas Zaidi

Production Stephanie McConnell

Fact Checker Mark Harding

Proofreader Christine Stroyan

Indexer Hilary Bird

Commissioned Photography Ian O'Leary

Frank Lukasseck 15tl; Scott Portelli 17c;
Frauke Scholz 31br; Gerard Soury 16cr;
ullstein bild 37tr; Westend61 67tr.

Graciosa Resort: 85cl.

Museu da Horta: 26bl.

Museu do Pico: 11bl.

Photoshot: Franco Banfi 40b; LOOK/Reinhard
Dirscherl 50tl, /Thomas Stankiewicz 11crb;
NHPA/Franco Banfi 24r.

Restaurant Anfiteatro: 54tr, 56c.

Gonçalo M. Rosa: 73tc.

SuperStock: age fotostock /David Muscroft
10cra, /Juan Carlos Muñoz 90tr; Mauritius/
Obert 30cla.

WestCanyon Turismo Aventura: 51cl.

Cover

Front and spine: **4Corners:** Günter
Gräfenhain.

Back: **Dreamstime.com:** Darksideofpink.

Pull Out Map Cover

4Corners: Günter Gräfenhain

All other images © Dorling Kindersley

For further information see:
www.dkimages.com

Penguin
Random
House

Printed and bound in China

First American Edition, 2017
Published in the United States by
DK Publishing, 345 Hudson Street,
New York, New York 10014

Copyright 2017 © Dorling
Kindersley Limited

A Penguin Random House Company

17 18 19 20 10 9 8 7 6 5 4 3 2 1

Published in Great Britain by Dorling
Kindersley Limited.

A catalog record for this book is available
from the Library of Congress.

ISSN 1479-344X
ISBN 978-1-4654-6064-6

MIX
Paper from
responsible sources
FSC FSC™ C018179
www.fsc.org

**SPECIAL EDITIONS OF
DK TRAVEL GUIDES**

*As a guide to abbreviations in visitor
information blocks:* **Adm** = *admission
charge;* **DA** = *disabled access.*

Phrase Book

In an Emergency

Help!	Socorro!	soo-koh-roo!
Stop!	Pára!	pahr'!
Call a doctor!	Chame um médico!	shahm'ooñ meh-dee-koo!
Call an ambulance!	Chame uma ambulância!	shahm'oo-muh añ-boo-lañ-see-uh!
Call the police!	Chame a polícia!	shahm'uh poo-lee-see-uh!
Call the fire brigade!	Chame os bombeiros!	shahm'oosh bom-bay-roosh!
Where is the nearest telephone?	Há um telefone aqui perto?	ah ooñ te-le-fon' uh-kee pehr-too?
Where is the nearest hospital?	Onde é o hospital mais próximo?	ond'eh oo ohsh-pee-tahl' mysh pro-see-moo?

Communication Essentials

Yes	Sim	seeñ
No	Não	nowñ
Please	Por favor/ Se faz favor	poor fuh-vor se-fash fuh-vor
Thank you	Obrigado/da	o-bree-gah-doo/duh
Excuse me	Desculpe	dish-koolp'
Hello	Olá	oh-lah
Goodbye	Adeus	a-deh-oosh
Good morning	Bom dia	boñ dee-uh
Good afternoon	Boa tarde	boh-uh tard'
Good night	Boa noite	boh-uh noyt'
Yesterday	Ontem	oñ-tayñ
Today	Hoje	ohj'
Tomorrow	Amanhã	ah-mañ yañ
Here	Aqui	uh-kee
There	Ali	uh-lee
What?	O quê?	oo keh?
Which?	Qual?	kwahl'?
When?	Quando?	kwañ-doo?
Why?	Porquê?	poor-keh?
Where?	Onde?	oñd'?

Useful Phrases

How are you?	Como está?	koh-moo shtah?
Very well, thank you	Bem, obrigado/da	bayñ, o-bree gah-doo/duh
Pleased to meet you	Encantado/a	eñ-kañ-tah-doo/duh
See you soon	Até logo	uh-teh loh-goo
That's fine	Está bem	shtah bayñ
Where is/are…?	Onde está/ estão…?	ond' shtah/ shtowñ…?
How far is it to…?	A que distância fica…?	uh kee dish-tañ-see-uh fee-kuh…?
Which way to…?	Como se vai para…?	koh-moo seh vy puh-ruh…?
Do you speak English?	Fala Inglês?	fah-luh eeñ-glehsh?
I don't understand	Não compreendo	nowñ kom-pree-eñ-doo
I'm sorry	Desculpe	dish-koolp'
Could you speak more slowly, please?	Pode falar mais devagar, por favor?	pohd' fuh-lar mysh d'-va-gar, poor fah-vor?

Useful Words

big	grande	grañd'
small	pequeno	pe-keh-noo
hot	quente	keñt'
cold	frio	free-oo
good	bom	boñ
bad	mau	mah-oo
enough	bastante	bash-tañt'
well	bem	bayñ
open	aberto	a-behr-too
closed	fechado	fe-shah-doo
left	esquerda	shkehr-duh
right	direita	dee-ray-tuh
straight on	em frente	ayñ freñt'
near	perto	pehr-too
far	longe	loñj'
up	suba	soo-bah
down	desça	deh-shuh
early	cedo	seh-doo
late	tarde	tard'
entrance	entrada	eñ-trah-duh
exit	saída	sa-ee-duh
toilets	casa de banho	kah-zuh d' bañ-yoo
more	mais	mysh
less	menos	meh-noosh

Making a Telephone Call

I would like to place an international call	Queria fazer uma chamada internacional	kree-uh fuh-zehr oo-muh sha-mah-duh in-ter-na-see-oo-nahl'
a local call	uma chamada local	oo-muh sha-mah-duh loo-kahl'
Can I leave a message?	Posso deixar uma mensagem?	poh-soo day-shar oo-muh meñ-sah-jayñ?

Shopping

How much does this cost?	Quanto custa isto?	kwañ-too koosh-tuh eesh-too?
I would like…	Queria…	kree-uh…
I'm just looking	Estou só a ver obrigado/a	shtoh soh uh vehr o-bree-gah-doo/uh
Do you take credit cards?	Aceita cartões de crédito?	uh-say-tuh kar-toinsh de kreh-dee-too?
What time do you open?	A que horas abre?	uh kee oh-rash ah-bre?
What time do you close?	A que horas fecha?	uh kee oh-rash fay-shuh?
this one	este	ehst'
that one	esse	ehss'
expensive	caro	kah-roo
cheap	barato	buh-rah-too
size (clothes/ shoes)	número	noom'-roo
white	branco	brañ-koo
black	preto	preh-too
red	vermelho	ver-melh-yoo
yellow	amarelo	uh-muh-reh-loo
green	verde	vehrd'
blue	azul	uh-zool'

Types of Shop

antique shop	loja de antiguidades	*loh-juh de añ-tee-gwee-dahd'sh*
bakery	padaria	*pah-duh-ree-uh*
bank	banco	*bañ-koo*
bookshop	livraria	*lee-vruh-ree-uh*
butcher	talho	*tah-lyoo*
cake shop	pastelaria	*pash-te-luh-ree-uh*
chemist	farmácia	*far-mah-see-uh*
fishmonger	peixaria	*pay-shuh-ree-uh*
hairdresser	cabeleireiro	*kab'-lay-ray-roo*
market	mercado	*mehr-kah-doo*
newsagent	quiosque	*kee-yohsk'*
post office	correios	*koo-ray-oosh*
shoe shop	sapataria	*suh-puh-tuh-ree-uh*
supermarket	supermercado	*soo-pehr-mer-kah-doo*
tobacconist	tabacaria	*tuh-buh-kuh-ree-uh*
travel agency	agência de viagens	*uh-jen-see-uh de vee-ah-jayñsh*

Sightseeing

cathedral	sé	*seh*
church	igreja	*ee-gray-juh*
garden	jardim	*jar-deeñ*
library	biblioteca	*bee-blee-oo-teh-kuh*
museum	museu	*moo-zeh-oo*
tourist information	posto de turismo	*posh-too d' too-reesh-moo*
closed for holidays	fechado para férias	*fe-sha-doo puh-ruh feh-ree-ash*
bus station	estação de autocarros	*shta-sowñ d' oh-too-kah-roosh*
railway station	estação de comboios	*shta-sowñ d' koñ-boy-oosh*
painted ceramic tile	azulejo	*uh-zoo-lay-joo*
Manueline (late Gothic architectural style)	manuelino	*ma-noo-el-ee-oo*

Staying in a Hotel

Do you have a vacant room?	Tem um quarto livre?	*tayñ ooñ kwar-too leevr'?*
room with a bath	um quarto com casa de banho	*ooñ kwar-too koñ kah-zuh d' bañ-yoo*
shower	duche	*doosh*
single room	quarto individual	*kwar-too een-dee-vee-doo-ahl'*
double room	quarto de casal	*kwar-too d' kuh-zhal'*
twin room	quarto com duas camas	*kwar-too koñ doo-ash kah-mash*
porter	porteiro	*poor-tay-roo*
key	chave	*shahv'*
I have a reservation	Tenho um quarto reservado	*tayñ-yoo ooñ kwar-too re-ser-vah-doo*

Eating Out

Have you got a table for...?	Tem uma mesa para...?	*tayñ oo-muh meh-zuh puh-ruh?*
I would like to reserve a table	Quero reservar uma mesa	*keh-roo re-zehr-var oo-muh meh-zuh*
The bill, please	A conta por favor/se faz favor	*uh kohn-tuh poor fuh-vor/ se-fash fuh-vor*
I am a vegetarian	Sou vegetariano/a	*Soh ve-je-tuh-ree-ah-noo/uh*
Waiter!	Por favor!/ Se faz favor!	*poor fuh-vor!/ se-fash fuh-vor!*
the menu	a lista	*uh leesh-tuh*
fixed-price menu	a ementa turística	*uh ee-mehñ-tuh too-reesh-tee-kuh*
wine list	a lista de vinhos	*uh leesh-tuh de veeñ-yoosh*
glass	um copo	*ooñ koh-poo*
bottle	uma garrafa	*oo-muh guh-rah-fuh*
half-bottle	meia-garrafa	*may-uh guh-rah-fuh*
knife	uma faca	*oo-muh fah-kuh*
fork	um garfo	*ooñ gar-foo*
spoon	uma colher	*oo-muh kool-yair*
plate	um prato	*ooñ prah-too*
breakfast	pequeno-almoço	*pe-keh-noo-ahl-moh-soo*
lunch	almoço	*ahl-moh-soo*
dinner	jantar	*jan-tar*
cover	couvert	*koo-vehr*
starter	entrada	*eñ-trah-duh*
main course	prato principal	*prah-too prin-see-pahl'*
dish of the day	prato do dia	*prah-too doo dee-uh*
set dish	combinado	*koñ-bee-nah-doo*
half-portion	meia-dose	*may-uh doh-se*
dessert	sobremesa	*soh-bre-meh-zuh*
rare	mal passado	*mahl' puh-sah-doo*
medium	médio	*meh-dee-oo*
well done	bem passado	*bayñ puh-sah-doo*

Menu Decoder

abacate	*uh-buh-kaht'*	avocado
açorda	*uh-sor-duh*	bread-based stew (often seafood)
açúcar	*uh-soo-kar*	sugar
água mineral	*ah-gwuh mee-ne-rahl'*	mineral water
alho	*ay-oo*	garlic
alperce	*ahl'-pehrce*	apricot
amêijoas	*uh-may-joo-ash*	clams
ananás	*uh-nuh-nahsh*	pineapple
arroz	*uh-rohsh*	rice
assado	*uh-sah-doo*	baked
atum	*uh-tooñ*	tuna
aves	*ah-vesh*	poultry
azeite	*uh-zayt'*	olive oil
azeitonas	*uh-zay-toh-nash*	olives
bacalhau	*buh-kuh-lyow*	dried, salted cod
banana	*buh-nah-nuh*	banana
batatas	*buh-tah-tash*	potatoes
batatas fritas	*buh-tah-tash free-tash*	French fries

batido	*buh-**tee**-doo*	milkshake
bica	***bee**-kuh*	espresso
bife	***beef***	steak
bolacha	*boo-**lah**-shuh*	biscuit
bolo	***boh**-loo*	cake
borrego	*boo-**reh**-goo*	lamb
caça	***kah**-ssuh*	game
café	*kuh-**feh***	coffee
camarões	*kuh-muh-**roysh***	large prawns
caracóis	*kuh-ruh-**koysh***	snails
caranguejo	*kuh-**rañ** **gay**-yoo*	crabs
carne	***karn**'*	meat
cataplana	*kuh-tuh-**plah**-nah*	sealed wok used to steam dishes
cebola	*se-**boh**-luh*	onion
cerveja	*sehr-**vay**-juh*	beer
chá	***shah***	tea
cherne	***shern**'*	stone bass
chocolate	*shoh-koh-**laht**'*	chocolate
chocos	***shoh**-koosh*	cuttlefish
chouriço	*shoh-**ree**-soo*	red, spicy sausage
churrasco	*shoo-**rash**-coo*	on the spit
cogumelo	*koo-goo-**meh**-loo*	mushroom
cozido	*koo-**zee**-doo*	boiled
enguias	*eñ-**gee**-ash*	eels
fiambre	*fee-**añbr**'*	ham
fígado	***fee**-guh-doo*	liver
frango	***frañ**-goo*	chicken
frito	***free**-too*	fried
fruta	***froo**-tuh*	fruit
gambas	***gañ**-bash*	prawns
gelado	*je-**lah**-doo*	ice cream
gelo	***jeh**-loo*	ice
goraz	*goo-**rash***	bream
grelhado	*grel-**yah**-doo*	grilled
iscas	***eesh**-kash*	marinated liver
lagosta	*luh-**gohsh**-tuh*	lobster
laranja	*luh-**rañ**-juh*	orange
leite	***layt**'*	milk
limão	*lee-**mowñ***	lemon
limonada	*lee-moo-**nah**-duh*	lemonade
linguado	*leeñ-**gwah**-doo*	sole
lulas	***loo**-lash*	squid
maçã	*muh-**sañ***	apple
manteiga	*mañ-**tay**-guh*	butter
marisco	*muh-**reesh**-koo*	seafood
meia-de-leite	***may**-uh-d'**layt**'*	white coffee
ostras	***osh**-trash*	oysters
ovos	***oh**-voosh*	eggs
pão	***powñ***	bread
pastel	*pash-**tehl**'*	cake
pato	***pah**-too*	duck
peixe	***paysh**'*	fish
peixe-espada	***paysh**'-**shpah**-duh*	scabbard fish
pimenta	*pee-**meñ**-tuh*	pepper
polvo	***pohl**'-voo*	octopus
porco	***por**-coo*	pork
queijo	***kay**-joo*	cheese
sal	***sahl**'*	salt
salada	*suh-**lah**-duh*	salad
salsichas	*sahl-**see**-shash*	sausages
sandes	***sañ**-desh*	sandwich
sopa	***soh**-puh*	soup
sumo	***soo**-moo*	juice
tamboril	*tañ-boo-**ril**'*	monkfish
tarte	***tart**'*	pie/cake
tomate	*too-**maht**'*	tomato
torrada	*too-**rah**-duh*	toast
tosta	***tohsh**-tuh*	toasted sandwich
vinagre	*vee-**nah**-gre*	vinegar
vinho branco	***veeñ**-yoo **brañ**-koo*	white wine
vinho tinto	***veeñ**-yoo **teeñ**-too*	red wine
vitela	*vee-**teh**-luh*	veal

Numbers

0	zero	*zeh-roo*
1	um	*ooñ*
2	dois	*doysh*
3	três	*tresh*
4	quatro	*kwa-troo*
5	cinco	*seeñ-koo*
6	seis	*saysh*
7	sete	*set'*
8	oito	*oy-too*
9	nove	*nov'*
10	dez	*desh*
11	onze	*oñz'*
12	doze	*doz'*
13	treze	*trez'*
14	catorze	*ka-torz'*
15	quinze	*keeñz'*
16	dezasseis	*de-zuh-**saysh***
17	dezassete	*de-zuh-**set**'*
18	dezoito	*de-**zoy**-too*
19	dezanove	*de-zuh-**nov**'*
20	vinte	*veent'*
21	vinte e um	*veen-**tee**-ooñ*
30	trinta	*treeñ-tuh*
40	quarenta	*kwa-**reñ**-tuh*
50	cinquenta	*seen-**kweñ**-tuh*
60	sessenta	*se-**señ**-tuh*
70	setenta	*se-**teñ**-tuh*
80	oitenta	*oy-**teñ**-tuh*
90	noventa	*noo-**veñ**-tuh*
100	cem	*sayñ*
101	cento e um	*señ-too-ee-**ooñ***
102	cento e dois	*señ-too-ee-**doysh***
200	duzentos	*doo-**zeñ**-toosh*
300	trezentos	*tre-**zeñ**-toosh*
400	quatrocentos	*kwa-troo-**señ**-toosh*
500	quinhentos	*kee-**nyeñ**-toosh*
600	seiscentos	*saysh-**señ**-toosh*
700	setecentos	*set'-**señ**-toosh*
800	oitocentos	*oy-too-**señ**-toosh*
900	novecentos	*nov'-**señ**-toosh*
1,000	mil	*meel'*

Time

one minute	um minuto	*ooñ mee-**noo**-too*
one hour	uma hora	*oo-muh **oh**-ruh*
half an hour	meia hora	*may-uh **oh**-ruh*
Monday	segunda-feira	*se-goon-duh-**fay**-ruh*
Tuesday	terça-feira	*ter-sa-**fay**-ruh*
Wednesday	quarta-feira	*kwar-ta-**fay**-ruh*
Thursday	quinta-feira	*keen-ta-**fay**-ruh*
Friday	sexta-feira	*say-shta-**fay**-ruh*
Saturday	sábado	*sah-ba-too*
Sunday	domingo	*doo-**meen**-goo*